GW00644827

IDENTITY SUITE

VISUAL IDENTITY IN STATIONERY

Edited and designed by viction:ary

VISUAL IDENTITY IN STATIONERY

IDENTITY SUITE

Published and distributed by
viction:workshop ltd.

viction:ary™

viction:workshop ltd.
Unit C, 7/F, Seabright Plaza, 9-23 Shell Street,
North Point, Hong Kong
Url: www.victionary.com   Email: we@victionary.com
www.facebook.com/victionworkshop
www.twitter.com/victionary_
www.weibo.com/victionary

Edited and produced by viction:workshop ltd.

Concepts & art direction by Victor Cheung
Book design by viction:workshop ltd.
Cover image by Bond
Imprint image by Anagrama

Second Edition
©2012, 2013 viction:workshop ltd.
Copyright on text and design work is held by respective
designers and contributors.

ISBN 978-988-19438-8-0

Printed and bound in China

IDENTITY SUITE

VISUAL IDENTITY IN STATIONERY

Edited and designed by viction:ary

MTLL

MTLL Arquitectos.
Arquitectura.Urbanismo.Landscape

Lázaro Garza – Ayala 169
T... ...6G
M...
CP 66240

...1) 833...61
www.mtllarqui...os.com
...@mtllarqui...os.com

FOREWORD
BY
ANAGRAMA

must be planned and executed to add up to the project's entropy. Each element will function in its own way adding up to the experience the client will have in each of the brand's contact points, shaping the general feelings the client has along the way. Each of the elements must be a good 'team-player'.

A brand is more than a simple company logo and corresponding stationery. Instead, a set of associations that consumers have in relation to your product, company, or service, seems more likely to define what a true brand is. One of the most important aspects that makes the difference between a simple brand and an excellent brand is its consistency.

We believe in consistency and do everything with our hands to achieve it. That is the cornerstone of branding. Consistency is about defining each part of the project so that it can be allowed to be in its own place with a defined objective adding up to the total project experience. Each of the elements of an identity, including stationery

Besides physical materials and identity you encounter when experiencing a brand, there are other important factors such as quality in the products and services, values transmitted by the people and customer service. When clients experiment that same level of quality, emotions and values again and again, your product, service and company will naturally stand out for it.

This is called branding.

FOREWORD BY DEUTSCHE & JAPANER

We understand visual identity and corporate design in a lively way. We lean towards developing it through different media with a pool of different elements, or a distinguished wardrobe if you would compare it with a closet of uniforms. Stiff manuals can limit the message, sometimes even appear to have lost touch of time. It's not about propagating anarchist design. Rules can be precious but approaching every medium and task with its own focus without a dogmatic system can make sense. A profound understanding of the client and his/her effort is crucial to deciding on and designing the right lexicon that is uniquely fit for a certain brand image and context.

From our point of view, this task can be met through developing a flexible range, a vocabulary, a grown family of media, birds of a feather. This is a philosophy that can keep the tension to every created matter — a shop, a compliment card or a sound. Although additional work and expense might be inevitable, it will pay off because of the higher level of attention and spirit inserted. Media always face different cultural and physical circumstances, be it touchable and present in forms of fragrance or physical objects; or totally immaterial, if you think of TV or web solutions that are currently reduced to an auditory and visual impulse. Identities can be seen through different lenses and perspectives (think of a foreign country with different rules and habits). Although it is possible to just follow the defaults, like employing a certain typeface, the exact corporate colours, margins, positions etc., we prefer the debate, followed by environmental adaptation, rather than finishing the job by sticking to the manual.

If we are thinking corporate communication or identity, it is all about the essence of character brought to life through paper or pixels. Clear objective targets on the one hand, but in best case honest descriptions close to the clients nature on the other. Corporate means expressing personality after principles and clarifications, not a paradigm of rigorous precision.

Corporate identity and stationery design is all about communicating a company's values and positioning with simple elements. On the web or in a brochure you can say it with words, images and graphics over many pages. But on a business card you need to say those things with simpler elements, like logo, typeface, colour and paper. Just the choice of paper, materials and print embellishments can reveal it all in a subtle way.

We strive to make identities and stationery packages that are sustainable, something that you want to hang on to, not to throw away into the closest garbage bin. At this time and age, standing out might be more important than ever. But in the end you don't want to be the one who is obviously and desperately crying out for attention in the crowd. It's about the small surprises and nifty details that carry the message of the concept — be it a custom typeface, surprising choice of material or an envelope displaying a new way of thinking. In addition to that, a unique, customised and useful extra materialisation will always lift an identity to new heights.

When working on an identity we try to cut down the unnecessary graphic elements, ask "Do we really need this?", and boil it down to the simplest elements that convey the concept without loosing personality and identity. Both in a communication point of view and a sustainable one, cutting down on unnecessary elements can lead to great things.

FOREWORD
BY
LARS KJELSNES
HEYDAYS

NEW DIRECTIONS IN STATIONERY

Bar corporate logos and company staff, stationery is the most accessible touch points between companies and their clients. As when every committed entrepreneur deserves a real decent identity to speak their character and mind, designers know well how stationery can be the perfect medium to impart aspirations and make some noise.

ALTITUDE MUSIC

by **& SMITH**

Independent production music library, Altitude Music, offers a profusion of copyrighted music for media use. While efficiency comes first for its patrons, much creative attention has been paid to its album catalogue, where genres and content are made explicit at first sight. A bold logotype unites Altitude's identity in additive colour primaries suggestive of a typical CRT display.

LOCATION/
London, UK
NATURE/
Production Music Library
PHOTO/
Richard Paul

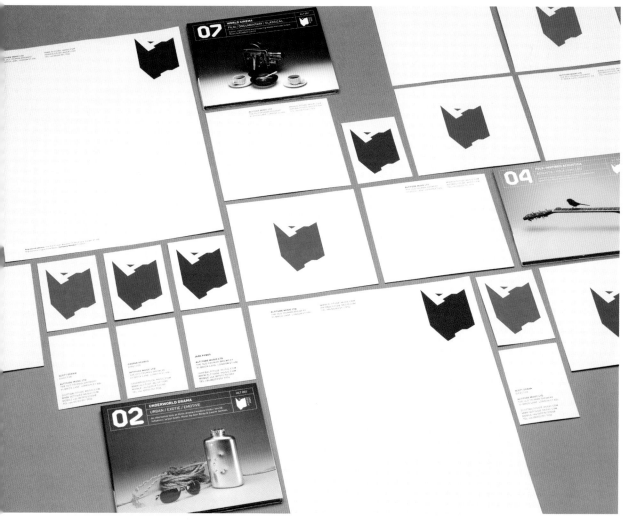

SUGARSIN

by **& SMITH**

SugarSin's sweets and desserts are for everyone, not just kids. Looking for a distinctly modern appearance, the store conceives an illustration-led brand image that talks to customers of all ages. A collage made of black-and-white illustrations and spirited features is applied across SugerSin's pick'n mix bags, business cards, pastry box and ice-cream tub, with a lollipop-inspired marque.

LOCATION/
London, UK
NATURE/
Confectionery Shop

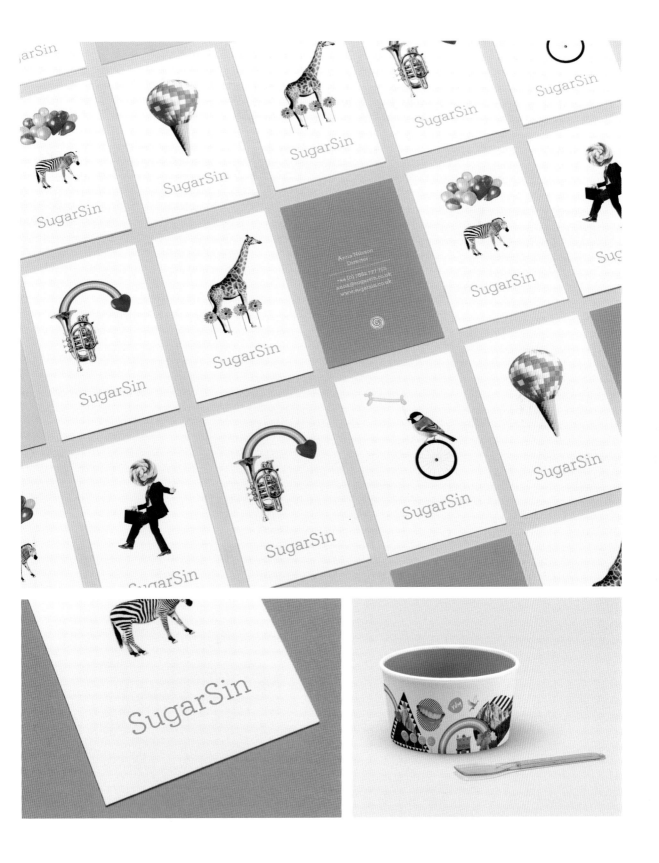

BRICOS

by **Anagrama**

BRICOS resolves to be a construction material supplier with much diligence, and an employer of which employees feel proud. Using bold slashes as the leitmotif of the entire design, the clean typographic language and institutional pattern are designed to communicate a sense of honesty, responsibility and experience that has been key to BRICOS' success throughout the years.

LOCATION/
Monterrey, Mexico
NATURE/
Construction Material
Supplier

MARÍA VOGEL

by **Anagrama**

Solid and sober, the monochrome visual identity subtly portrays the Latin-American fashion designer's attitude and mature eyes on her garments that serve to be a real alternative to the world's foremost brands. Typeface "Vogel Display" was particularly crafted to reflect the brand's distinct character, with a simple piece of thread to relate garments to the brand.

LOCATION/
Monterrey, Mexico
NATURE/
Independent Fashion Designer

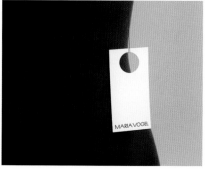

MTLL

by **Anagrama**

Founded by two experienced architects, MTLL wanted an identity to manifest their acute sense of architectural sensibility to offset its young history. The result is a typographic solution that imparts the duo's constant search of simplicity and pragmatism in architectural design. While the contrasting strokes of the logotype add strength to the brand, the serif details compensate for the illegibility with unique personality.

LOCATION/
San Pedro, Mexico
NATURE/
Architectural
Design Firm

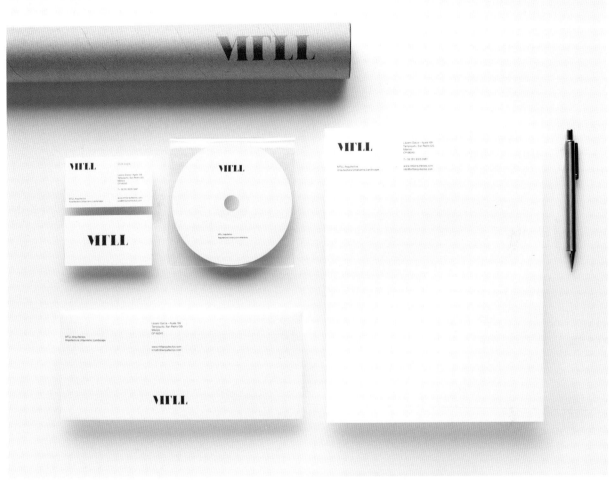

THE HUM-
MINGBIRD

by **Analogue**

The Hummingbird is a three-storey kitchen-and-bar in which the region's finest local produce and cocktails can be found. For a more warm and rustic experience, Analogue formulated a unique identity through art direction, organic paper, bespoke clipboards and an exotic colouration reflecting the bird's signature plumage. Its steel signage showing a combined character in assorted typeface is expected to rust and add to its personality over time.

LOCATION/
Leeds, UK
NATURE/
Casual Dining
Restaurant
PHOTO/
Rob Booker

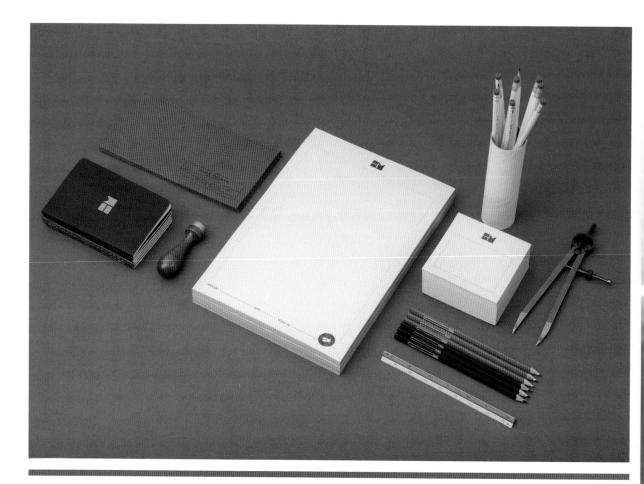

HILLE MELBYE

by **ANTI**

Hille Melbye Arkitekter was experiencing a change of generation, with the addition of young architects who were daring to think different and take the firm to the forefront of the Norwegian architectural scene. Commissioned to design a visually powerful logo to brand their communications and design, ANTI came up with a direct solution that played on space. The logo depicted the firm's initials in its negative space as a reference to the architects' everyday task.

LOCATION/
Oslo, Norway
NATURE/
Architectural
Design Firm

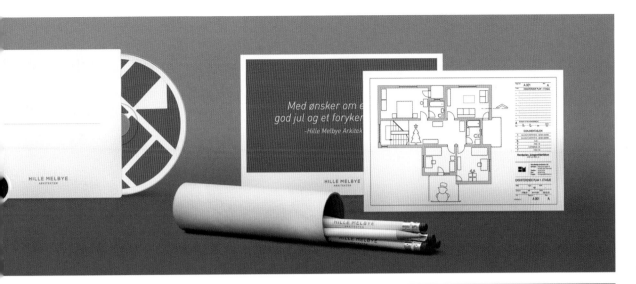

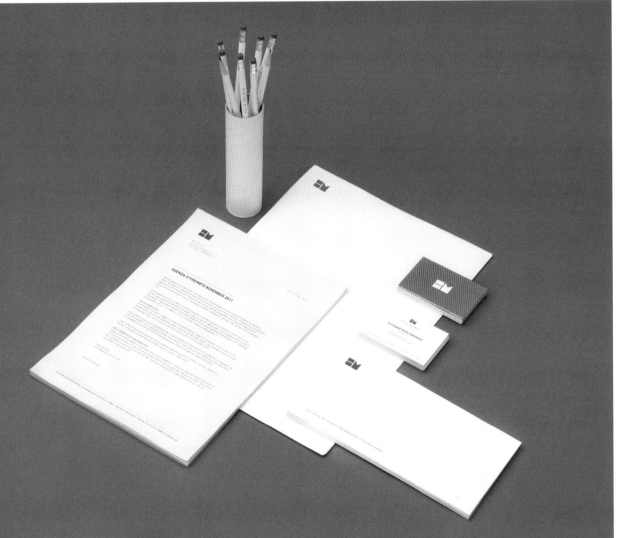

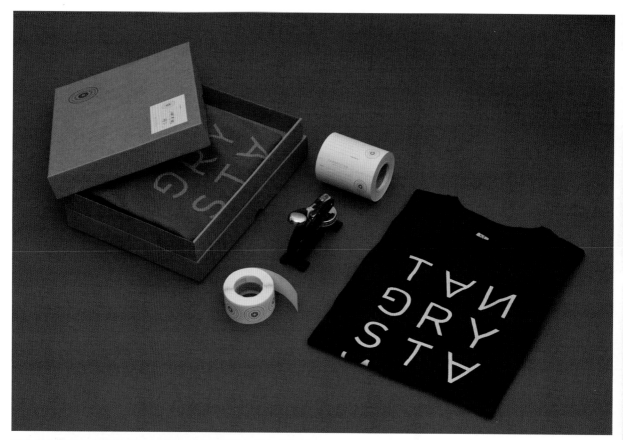

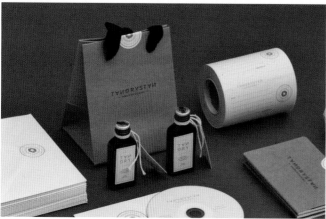

TANGRYSTAN

by **ANTI**

Tangrystan is a place with its own culture, in which everyone takes pride in filming TV-commercials imbued with new ideas and a great sense of Norwegian humour. While the pronunciation of its name gives a subtle association with the Balkans, the identity accentuated the sensation alongside their work-play attitude with a touch of dusty pink.

LOCATION/
Oslo, Norway
NATURE/
Production Firm

TRIGGER
OSLO

by **ANTI**

Trigger Oslo is a new public relations company specialising in engaging marketing and communications. Where good conversations begin with a warm and cozy atmosphere, ANTI dressed Trigger in a range of personal signatures made of simple graphics on paper and apparels unified by a bright and candid character in an orange tone.

LOCATION/
Oslo, Norway
NATURE/
Public Relations Firm

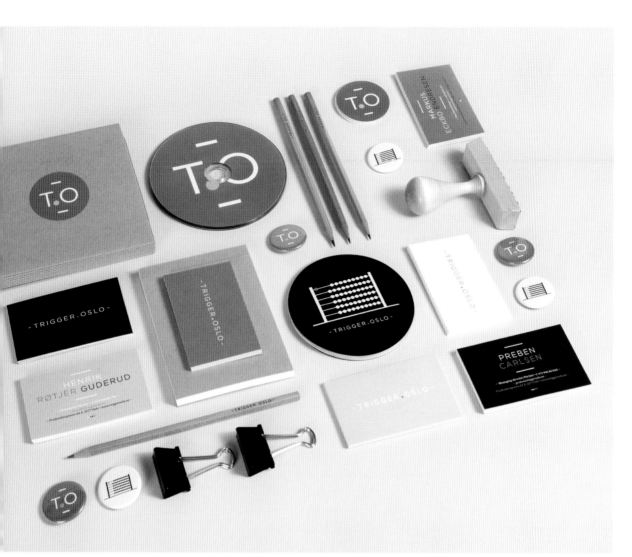

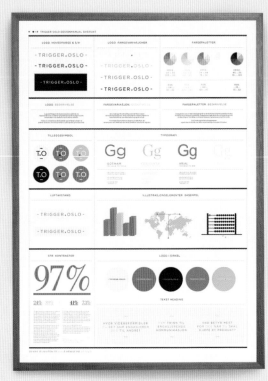

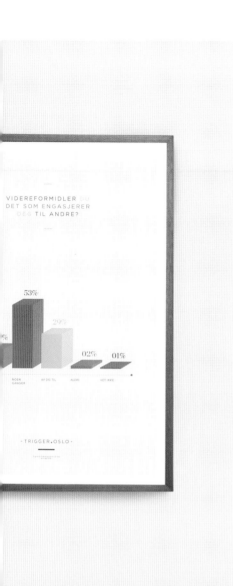

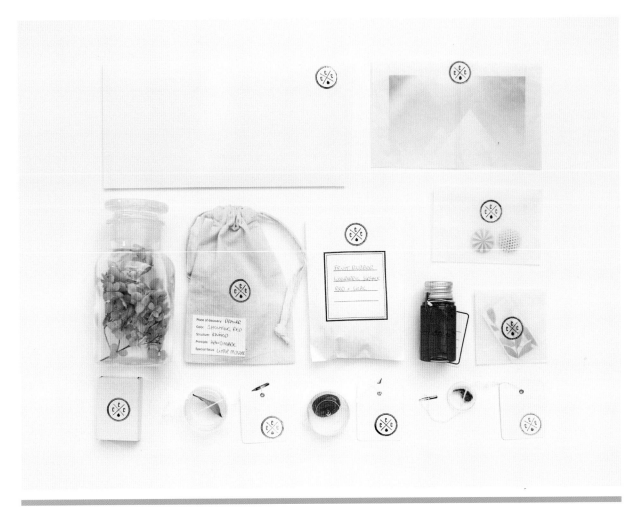

COME
CLOSER
CLUB

by **ARE WE DESIGNER**

Every year BASF Coatings assembles its major clients in the automotive industry to find out about their latest colour collections in form of a 'colour show'. For year 2011, the event was imagined as a private club, where honourable members were invited to bring along their favourite items with great colour impressions to show and discuss at the venue. The invitation kit contained a pin with the club's emblem and a box with vessels to display their finds.

LOCATION/
Ludwigshafen,
Germany
NATURE/
Coating Firm

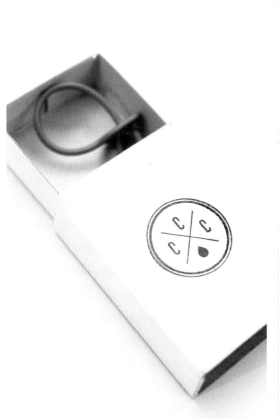

TOMOMI

by **ARE WE DESIGNER**

ARE WE DESIGNER was approached by a friend to create a full-range visual identity package for her start-up fashion flagship shop. 'TO-MOMI' was adopted as the name for its connection with 'friendship' and 'beauty' in Japanese context, followed by a series of origami-inspired designs to boost its Japanese sensation. Colourful ribbons, stickers and wrappers were added to double the fun while shopping at the store.

LOCATION/
Cologne, Germany
NATURE/
Fashion Boutique

ATIPO

by **atipo**

The strength of atipo's identity lies totally in the typography, a solid geometrical sans serif with a humanistic touch identified as 'atipo sans'. Also available in light and regular weights, atipo sans displays an exceptional quality in its graphic edits that merit an absolutely clean background to set off. Selective signs are singled out on the back of their letters that could as well work as posters to decorate the wall.

LOCATION/
Asturias, Spain
NATURE/
Graphic Design House

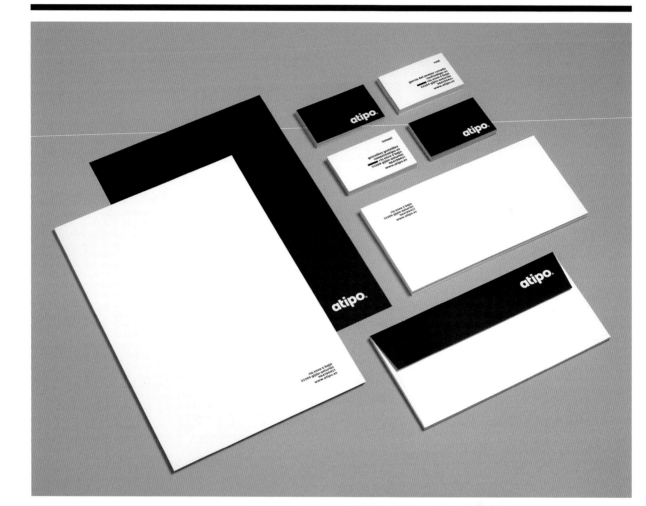

light
regular
bøld

atipo sans
abcdefghijklmnñopqrstuvwxyz
0123456789 $£¥€ƒ
&#%‰†‡@®©™ªº*

type

finely tuned in hi...
mechanical an...
shapes.
as a clean...

EDITIONS
OF 100

by **BERG**

Suggested by its name, Editions of 100 is a gallery and outlet for original limited edition items with a stock of 100. Operated by BERG in hands with a cluster of artists, designers and photographers, the cyber store and its internal documentation offer a neutral background to accentuate the prints. A fluorescent green overprint is designed to pop and greet the potential buyers on the tote bag, as well as the website as they enter the page.

LOCATION/
Glasgow, UK
NATURE/
E-commerce Portal

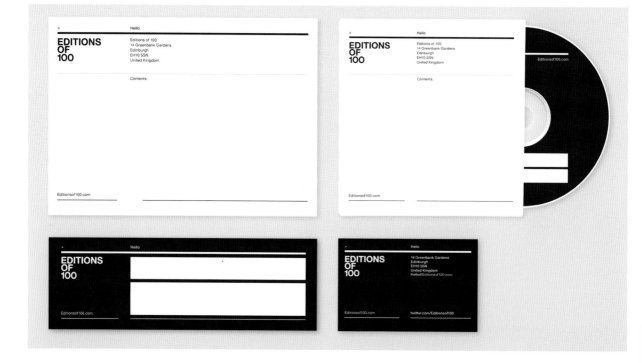

> **EDITIONS OF 100**

Editionsof100.com

Original limited edition prints: Art, Design & Photography

THE GUILD

by **BERG**

Consisted of parts, the logo of The Guild imparts their cooperative nature and diverse qualities in a nutshell. While the new animation and visual effects collective focuses on TV broadcasting, BERG drew inspirations from vintage tele graphics and typography, especially from those on monochromatic test cards, to create a tangible link to their expertise and variations for the brand.

LOCATION/
London, UK
NATURE/
Visual Effect Collective

THEGUILD.TV

THEGUILD.TV

THEGUILD.TV

LORNA

by **BERG**

All you need to know about Lorna is her outlandish approach to imagery which often projects a quirkiness almost equivalent to that in the Bothers Grimm, their dark Germanic fairytales and Tim Burton. Apart from the subtle hint of Victorian qualities in the palette and materials, BERG also composed a signature-logo to point to Lorna's flamboyant personality.

LOCATION/
UK
NATURE/
Photo-retouching
Technician

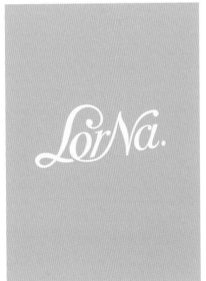

my curate create celebrate

MYSPACE

by **Bleed**

Simple yet iconic, the well-recognised symbol for "space" makes for a clever and exciting new look to take the already popular social publishing platform to a new engaging level. Graphically giving the brand a real room to grow, Bleed's choice for the combined elements communicates Myspace as a variable allowing everyone to be whoever they want. The idea is further visualised in a range of compositions randomly rendered with snapshots by members of Myspace or hired professionals.

LOCATION/
Los Angeles, US
NATURE/
Social Publishing
Platform

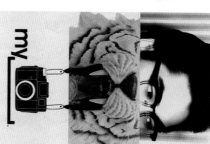

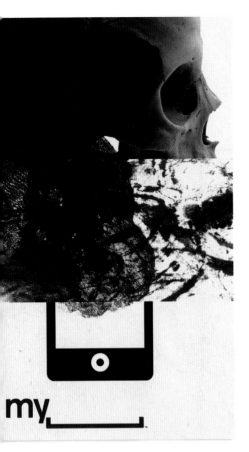

407 North Maple Drive, 2nd Floor
Beverly Hills, CA 90210

T +1 310.969.7856 / F +1 310.969.7388
myspace.com

407 North Maple Drive, 2nd Floor
Beverly Hills, CA 90210
myspace.com

ATTIDO

by **Bond**

Switching to a new identity with a new name, Attido has commissioned an overhaul of its brand appearance to cope with its globalising business in the competitive sphere of information system engineering. Building the brand using only black and yellow, the eye-catching combination communicates their dedication and goal-driven attitude. Their promise 'Until it's done' is solidified as it repeats on every touch point between Attido and their clients.

LOCATION/
Espoo, Finland
NATURE/
Information System Engineer

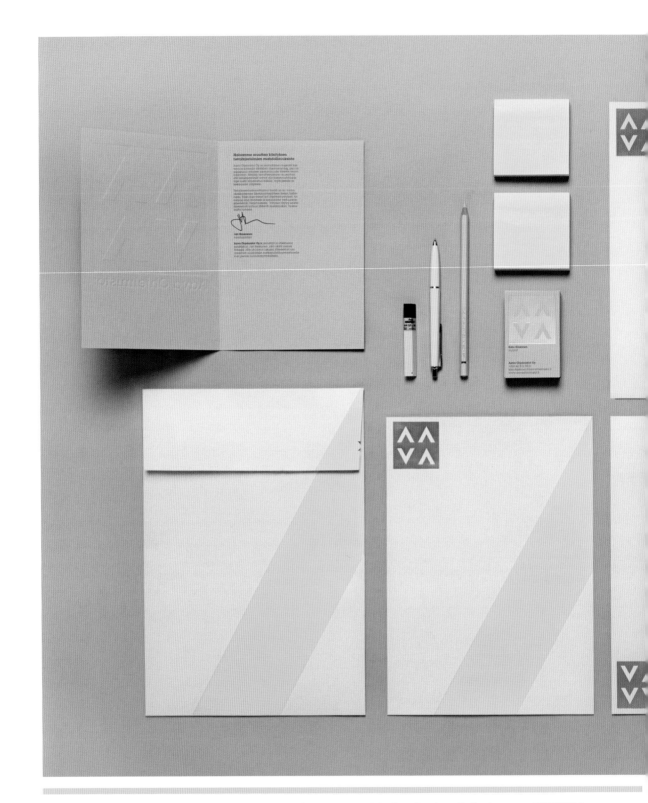

AAVA

by **Bond**

Inspired by Aava's unique letter combination, Bond capitalised on the similar forms of 'A' and 'V' to create a logotype that could as well evolve into simple yet small brand elements to brand its sales tools. The thick strokes stylishly strike through a variety of applications in blind-embossing and as print in bold yellow or metallic silver on zinc white paper stock.

LOCATION/
Espoo, Finland
NATURE/
IT Consulting Firm

Ota etumatkaa kilpailijoihisi

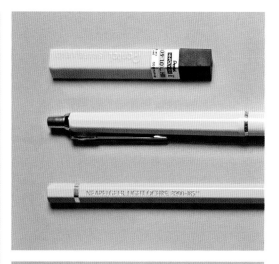

Karo Kiiskinen
myynti

Aava Ohjelmistot Oy
+358 40 512 5933
karo.kiiskinen@aavaohjelmistot.fi
www.aavaohjelmistot.fi

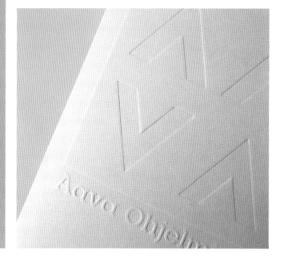

KAUFMANN
----

by **Bond**

Finnish marketing agency Kaufmann introduces a revolutionary market-driven mindset to help healthcare and welfare businesses expand. While traditional values also matter, a mixed typographic style is set to balance the old against the new. The agency's areas of expertise are specifically illustrated and rendered in a three-frame animation to enliven marketing concepts on Kaufmann's brand book and website.

LOCATION/
Helsinki, Finland
NATURE/
Marketing Agency

KESKO

by **Bond**

Trading sector service provider, Kesko has its hands in sectors as varied as food and cars. To promote the retail conglomerate's entrepreneurial culture and its multifaceted services, Bond injected a vibrant character into the 60-year-old enterprise with a cheerful palette. A type-based approach ensures brand dynamism within a time-resistant look.

LOCATION/
Helsinki, Finland
NATURE/
Retailing Conglomerate

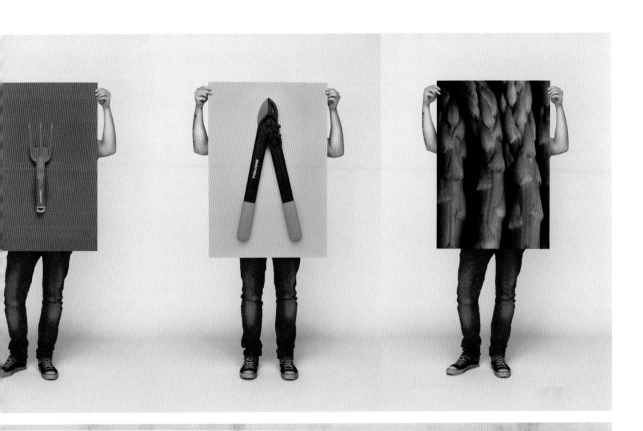

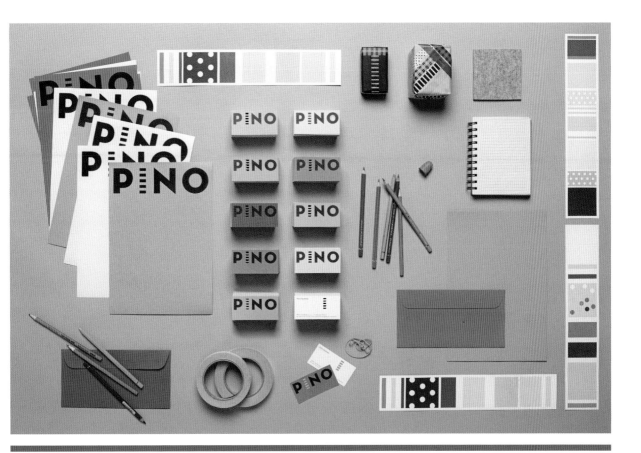

PINO

by **Bond**

This marketplace for handpicked lifestyle products has its store concept centred around its name 'PINO', Finnish for 'pile' or 'stack'. Visually embracing the idea into the shop's identity, Bond has the name 'PINO' prominently installed behind the counter with the 'I' made of wall shelves and of punctures on its business cards. The stationery set is rendered in a subtle yet voguish palette that echos the shop's personality and product range.

LOCATION/
Helsinki, Finland
NATURE/
Lifestyle Product
Retailer

FIVE & DIME
EATERY

by **Bravo Company**

Tied in with the eatery's name and idea of offering simple dine-in menus at an honest price, Five & Dime's visual identity takes on a retro-classic aesthetic and revolves around a circle, symbolic of coins that generally carry little monetary values. Branded stationery, such as expenditure pads and pencils, corresponding to the brand and the old-time frugal lifestyle are also created for sale at the store.

LOCATION/
Singapore, Singapore
NATURE/
Casual Dining
Restaurant

DEBBIE DOES

by **Brogen Averill,
Michael Hourigan**

Debbie does a lot of things! She is a specialist in multiple disciplines spanning corporate communications, strategic comms, human resources, investor relations and sustainability. To simplify her profile and bring focus back to her areas of knowledge for specific target clients, the letterhead starts the statement with a solid black "Debbie does" followed by an almost nude remark. Her particular expertise can also be identified by the different colour stock used.

3ANGRYMAN

by **Build**

From its trichromatic line pattern to its bracketed marque, all graphic elements are built to suggest the gadgets which 3angrymen, the digital production house, has to use everyday. Simple yet functional, the marque can be easily personalised by replacing the content of the brackets or adopted as a "corporate check-box" in the firm's letterheads and label templates. The stationery set also includes a double-sided A4 sheet to hold discs as it is folded into place.

LOCATION/
London, UK
NATURE/
Digital Production
House

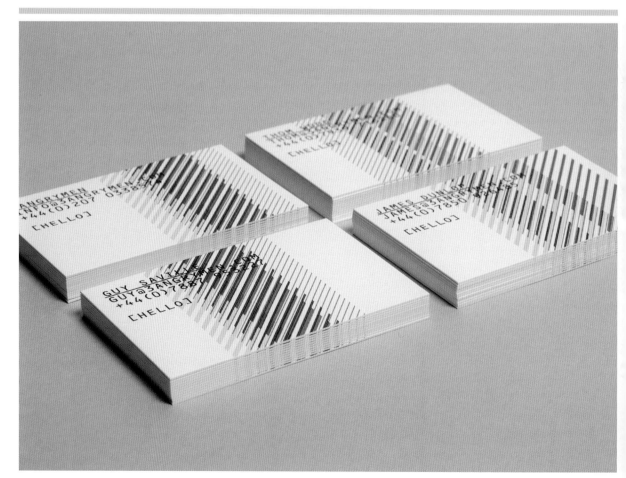

FEMA

by **Bureau Bruneau**
(Ludvig Bruneau Rossow)

The (fictional) U.S. Federal Emergency Management Agency is set up as a contingency plan for survivors of doomsday. With pragmatism in focus, lavish packaging and graphic elements are eschewed in FEMA's visual language system. The authority has its badge stamped on everything from instruction manuals to food supply to reinforce a sense of unity within the community.

NATURE/
Public Service
PHOTO/
John Tøsse Kolvik

B.R.

by **Bureau Rabensteiner**

B.R. represents Bureau Rabensteiner, who takes pleasure in tailoring creative concepts and art directions at their Innsbruck base. Hoping to keep their in-house stationery, even their daily utilities, simple and sleek, a monochrome aesthetic continues to dominate the design as it is in their workplace. For a vintage touch, they use a rubber stamp with a wood handle to denote special messages on corporate documents.

LOCATION/
Innsbruck, Austria
NATURE/
Graphic Design Firm

DEEP
SEARCH

by **Christian Bielke**

The newly established Norwegian shoe brand Deep Search emphasises an effective use of materials in shoe-making in addition to its quality cuts, seams and details. A coherent approach to complete Deep Search's concept is an identity with an earth tone scheme and an outlined logotype that requires minimal printing on recycled cartons. For an extra appeal, product cards are given away in kraft envelopes for every corresponding pair sold.

LOCATION/
Oslo, Norway
NATURE/
Shoe Manufacturer
PHOTO/
Henrik Beck Kæmpe

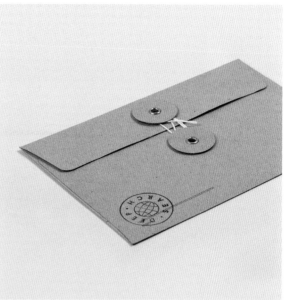

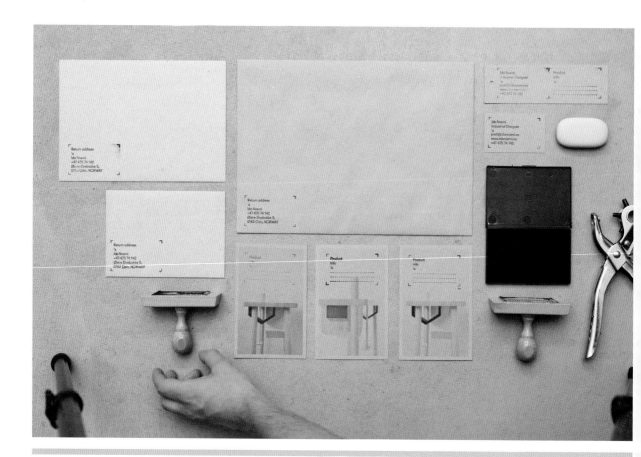

IDA NOEMI

by **Christian Bielke**

Ida Noemi is an industrial design graduate who needed a small-scale identity as she started freelancing. While the package was designed for easy and low-cost production, a remarkably straightforward solution with plain information and pictures enables Noemi to restyle her business card, stationery, product cards, mailing labels and hang tags with three simple stamps for whichever design or furniture fair she partakes.

LOCATION/
Oslo, Norway
NATURE/
Independent Industrial Designer
PHOTO/
Marius Nilsen

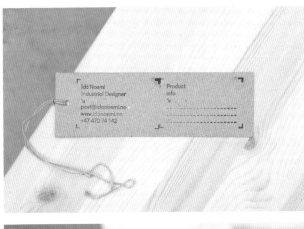

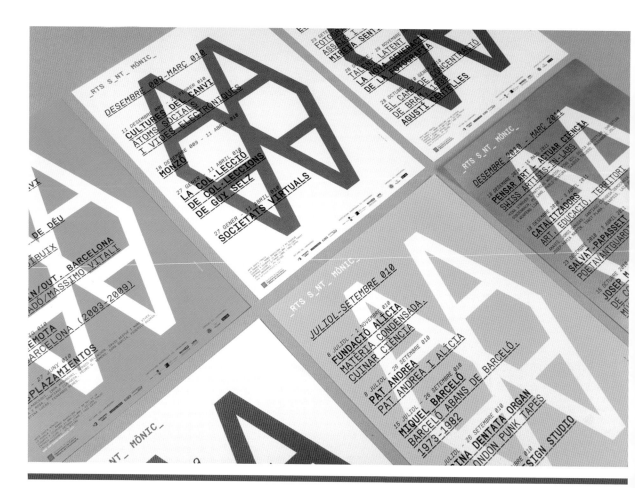

ARTS SANTA MÒNICA

by **clasebcn**

Contemporary art is not just about artistic creations at Arts Santa Mònica, but also science, thought and communication. To highlight the four equally important disciplines, clasebcn drew on the four As from the institution's name to create a symmetric logotype. The logotype repeatedly and prominently appears across the centre's space and collateral as decor, patterns and signage in eye-catching tones.

LOCATION/
Barcelona, Spain
NATURE/
Cultural Institution
LETTERING/
Íñigo Jerez

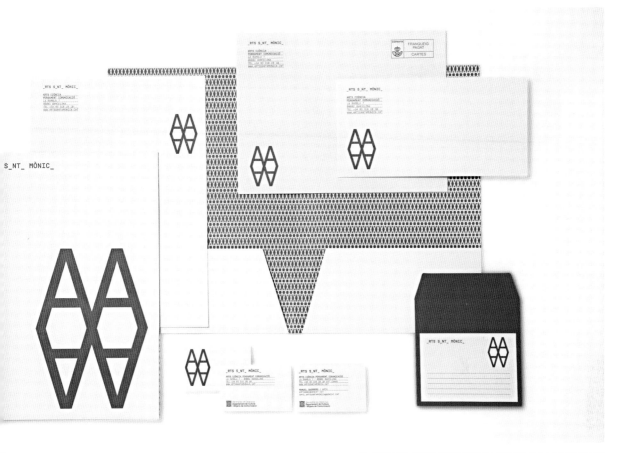

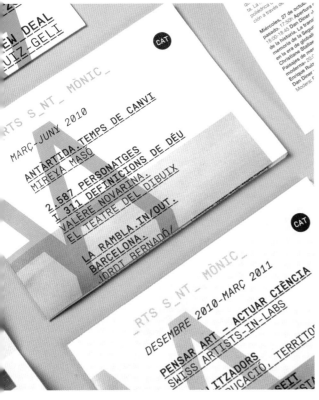

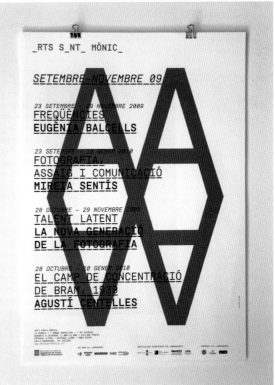

CLASEBCN

by **clasebcn**

Specialising in visual communication, clasebnc naturally saw the opportunity to display their creative talents while designing their own corporate stationery design. Their solution is a highly flexible system combining manufactured paper products and a variety of in-house graphic stickers, allowing the team to personalise communications and refresh their identity from time to time.

LOCATION/
Barcelona, Spain
NATURE/
Graphic Design Studio

SENTEURS D'AILLEURS

by **Codefrisko**

The original concept of Senteurs d'Ailleurs has always been its constant search for the sense of tradition and craftsmanship once associated with the art of perfume. Instead of a sole brand mark, Codefrisko created two massive ones with antique woodcut imagery and modernist shapes to narrate the kind of sophistication exclusive to its handmade product range. Rhombus is integral to the entire brand identity that extends to the boutique's retail design.

LOCATIOIN/
Brussels, Belgium
NATURE/
Fragrant & Skincare
Boutique

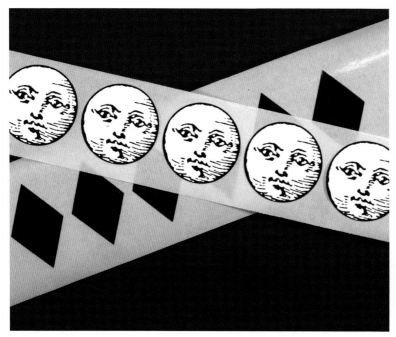

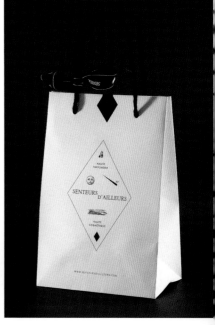

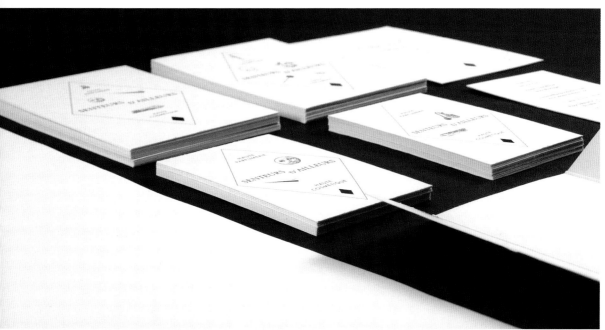

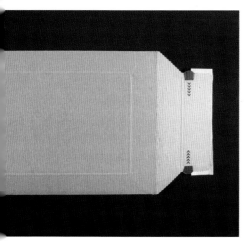

HECKER
GUTHRIE

by **Cornwell**

Led by Paul Hecker and Hamish Guthrie, Hecker Guthrie's interior projects are driven by the principle of authenticity that resonates not only in their design solutions but also the artistry, selection of materials and the natural palette. Crafted, detailed, textured, bold, tactile and sumptuous, the brand update celebrates their business evolution with a new name, new business cards, notepads and invitation cards to share the news with clients and friends.

LOCATION/
Melbourne, Australia
NATURE/
Interior Design Firm

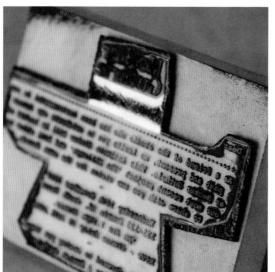

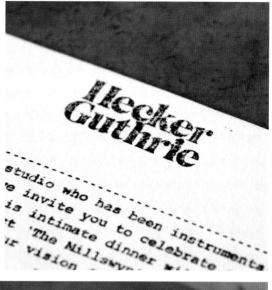

Hecker·
Guthrie

studio who has been instrumenta
e invite you to celebrate
is intimate dinner w
t 'The Millswyn
r vision

RUBEN
HESTHOLM

by **Daniel Brokstad**

Apart from photographic skills, a photographer's tool is also crucial to producing distinctive quality in pictures. For a modern language that talks to families, young lovers and the newly-wedded, a much straightforward character was composed for Hestholm using forms and colours commonly found on cameras. Specific items, such as the envelopes, business cards and CD sleeves, are tailored to tally with the measurements of his gear and encompassing mastery.

LOCATION/
Sandnes, Norway
NATURE/
Photographer

DEPARTE-
MENT

by **Departement**

The stationery set of creative studio Departement in Quebec gives an exceptional interpretation of minimalism using fiery colours and words muted in foil stamping and blind-embossing. Where each application stands out in its own fluorescent colour, the entire suite is set to be a quintessence of Departement's sensibility and style. Each business card comes in a small envelope with a short company profile imprint.

LOCATION/
Quebec, Canada
NATURE/
Design Studio

IGNANT

by **Deutsche & Japaner**

The versatile hexagon that denotes iGNANT in various faces is a synonym of the German blog's multidimensional approach and dedication to creative topics relevant to the general public. The shape has lent its geometric qualities to iGNANT's identity, forming its logo, corporate pattern and iconographic system to identify the different themes that guest authors randomly contribute to the blog.

LOCATION/
Berlin, Germany
NATURE/
Creative Blog

KÖNIG
BANSAH

by **Deutsche & Japaner**

Céphas Bansah, also known as King Bansah, resides in Ludwigshafen, Germany where he governs his subjects afar, operates a beer brand and makes frequent public and media appearances to fund and generate interest for his aid projects in Ghana. His new corporate design is a combination of royal identity and exotic impressions, as well as authenticity and lordliness — the backbone of the king's prestige and his charity projects.

LOCATION/
Ludwigshafen, Germany
NATURE/
Charity Project
PHOTO/
Mirka Laura Severa

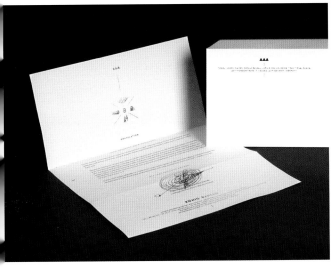
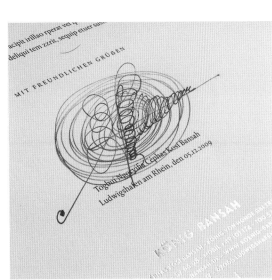
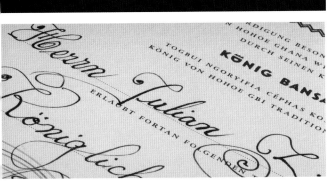
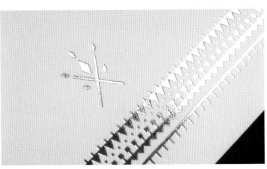

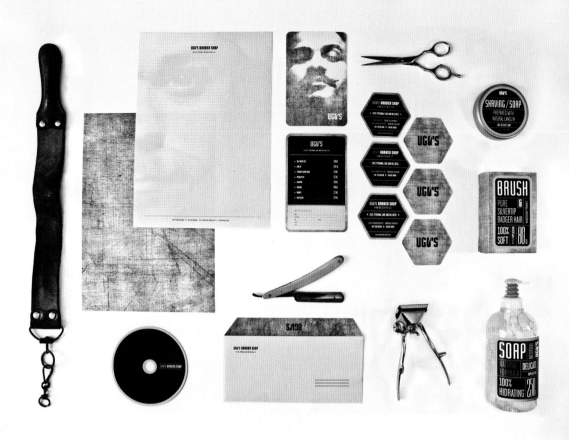

UGO'S BAR-
BER SHOP

by **Egidio Filippetti**

A promise of satisfaction that any man can possibly receive from Ugo's shop is inscribed in his logo with an accurate cut-out in the 'O' that also suggests the well-polished razor in his steady hands. A direct correlation between manliness and Ugo's cuts is further elaborated using raw prints, ice blue and cool greys on his stationery and packaging on a typographic base.

LOCATION/
Rome, Italy
NATURE/
Barber Shop

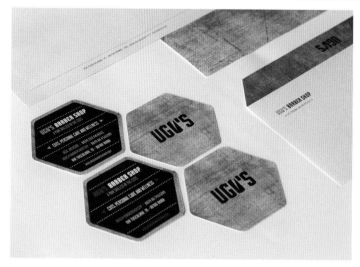

UGU'S
BARBER · SHOP

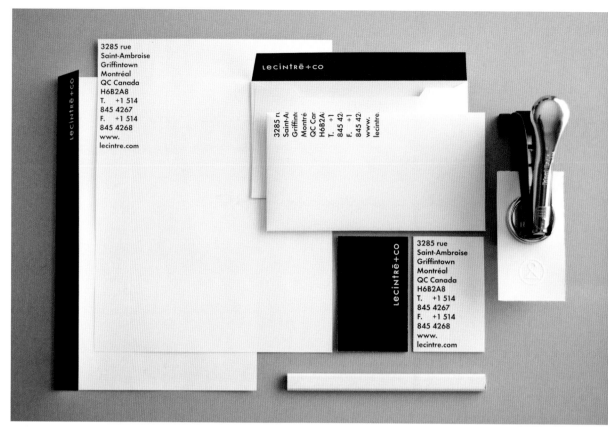

LE CINTRÉ
& CO.

by **Emanuel Cohen**

Le Cintré & Co. is an intermediate station for travellers and creative space for artists (its French name, meaning 'hanger' and 'arc' which offers architectural support spelled out in mixed type cases might give a hint). Just as the hotel gives priority to arts development and its guests, practical information acquires a relatively more prominent position on every touch point. The hotel's name only reveals as one opens the hotel envelope or flips over its letter or key cards.

LOCATION/
Quebec, Canada
NATURE/
Boutique Hotel
CONSULTATION/
Louis Gagnon

LAUGHING
MAN

by **Established**

Laughing Man is a charitable foundation driven by their "All Be Happy!" vision and promise to support agribusiness and developments in Ethiopia. Albeit its philanthropic orientation, the value of 'quality' remains in the details visible in the typeface, greytone and a dash of glam on selected identity pieces. The core idea of selling and consuming their ethically-sourced products is stressed with a variety of smiling faces to go on their packaging, as well as coffees and teas.

LOCATION/
New York, US
NATURE/
Charity Project

ROUND HILL MUSIC

by **Established**

The extensive use of bright pink masking tapes across Round Hill's identity refers to the tape's usual application in the music industry. While its spontaneous style conveys the management firm's great zest for music, the logo also takes advantage of the fact to spotlight the company's insider credentials and artist-friendly management style which is gaining prominence in the field. Real pink tape rolls are included in the package for practical use.

LOCATION/
New York, US
NATURE/
Music Management Firm

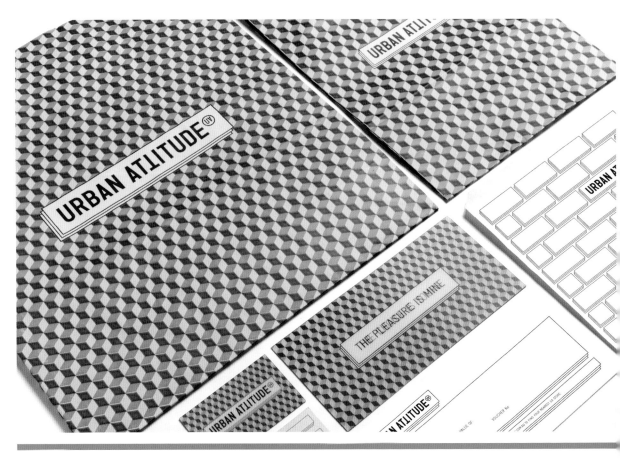

URBAN ATTITUDE

by **Fabio Ongarato Design**

The customised "trademark symbol" and the playful twist in the lettering is already showing you what Urban Attitude is about. With expansion plans following the introduction of new partners to the novelty store, the new flagship store required a brand update to epitomise the new dynamic urban chic. Compact patterns and lenticular printing were heavily employed across the shop's collateral suite, in line with its electric interior, streetscape flags and illuminated signage.

LOCATION/
Melbourne, Australia
NATURE/
Lifestyle Product Retailer
PHOTO/
Sharyn Cairns

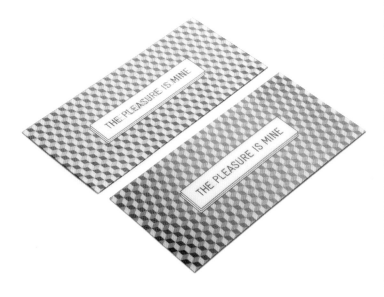

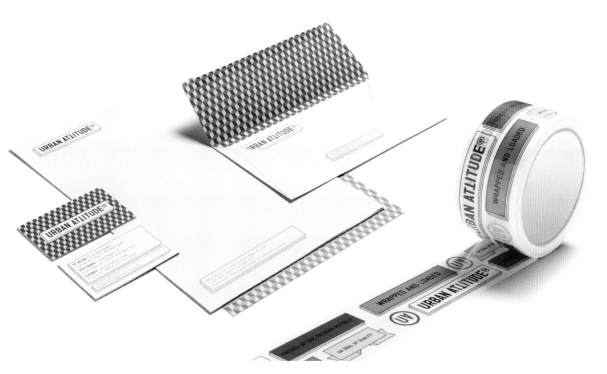

FILTHYMEDIA

by filthymedia

Print-based design studio filthymedia wanted to take full advantage of their stationery to showcase the value of print. With a latex logo embossed to contrast the uncoated paper stock and details, like a turquoise tint to accent the overall design, the result is an exhaustive approach that combines corporate beliefs, technical expertise and artistry within one single medium.

LOCATION/
Brighton, UK
NATURE/
Graphic Design Studio
PHOTO & PRINTING/
Generation Press

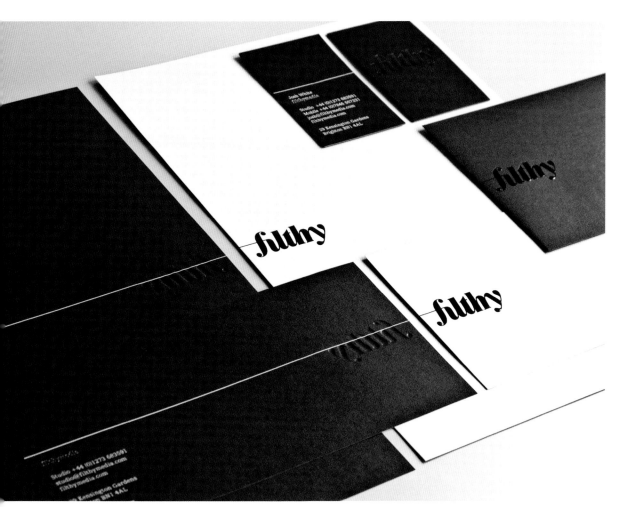

PLAYGROUND STUDIO

by **Foreign Policy Design Group**

Playground Studio is a music laboratory where music is part and parcel of life, even a storm can break out in notes. Business cards and letterheads are ink-stamped on recycled candy-colour paper easily obtainable from local stationers. All items can be reprinted on a need basis — a truly sustainable and green effort without exercising the printing press.

LOCATION/
Singapore, Singapore
NATURE/
Music Production Studio

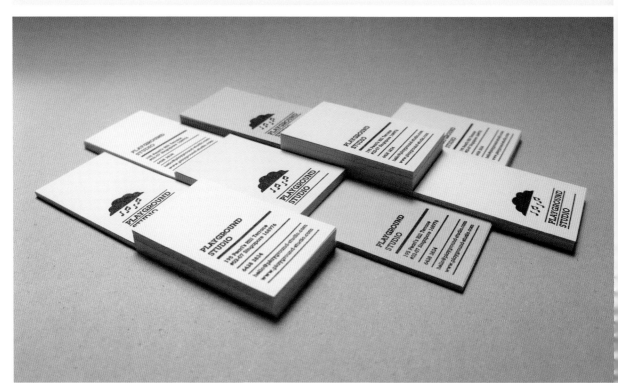

THE WATER-
HOUSE

by **Foreign Policy Design Group**

The brand identity of this new boutique hotel is founded on the concept of "duality" — like the old and the modern that coexist in the city, and the overall architectural design intent of inside out, outside in. Another layer of the identity pays tribute to the Waterhouse originally built as a warehouse. The graphic profile was built in squares to mimic the stacking and storage of cargo and goods.

LOCATION/
Shanghai, China
NATURE/
Boutique Hotel

REDBLUE
RESEARCH

by **Golden**

Mixing red and blue naturally gets purple. But Redblue is much more than that. They are a team of professionals good at providing carefully crafted qualitative and quantitative research solutions. Above and beyond the pertinent details on its stationery is a loud and clear shout of Redblue's manifestos and passion for research. The typeface also reflects a fun-loving spirit that sets the team apart from the rest.

LOCATION/
London, UK
NATURE/
Marketing & Research Consultancy
PHOTO/
Richard Moran

7TV

by **Greg Barth, Vanda Daftari, Capucine Labarthe**

The goal of this rebranding project was to boost the image of the Russian self-help TV channel. The identity approach was designed to yield a versatile character out of bold palettes, paired with visual tricks to fit its varied topics spanning travels, cinema, renovations and relationships. To correspond 7TV's idea that anyone can act to improve their life, all on-screen elements were assembled and animated by hand to relate to a human approach.

LOCATION/
Moscow, Russia
NATURE/
TV Channel
PHOTO RETOUCHING/
Visual Box

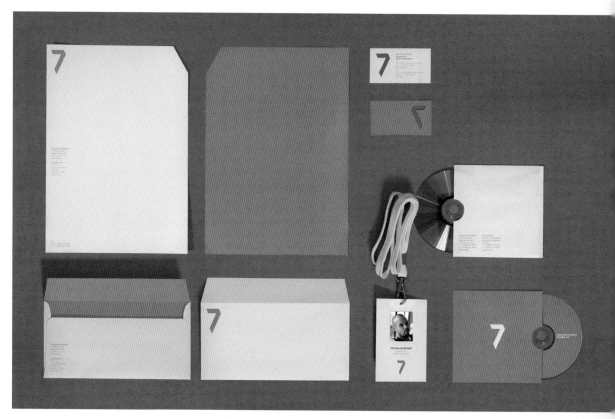

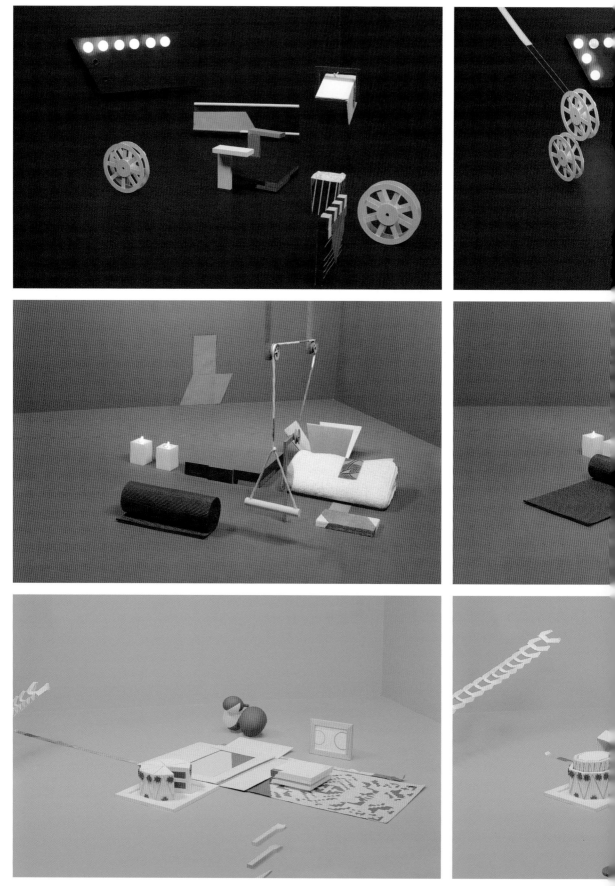

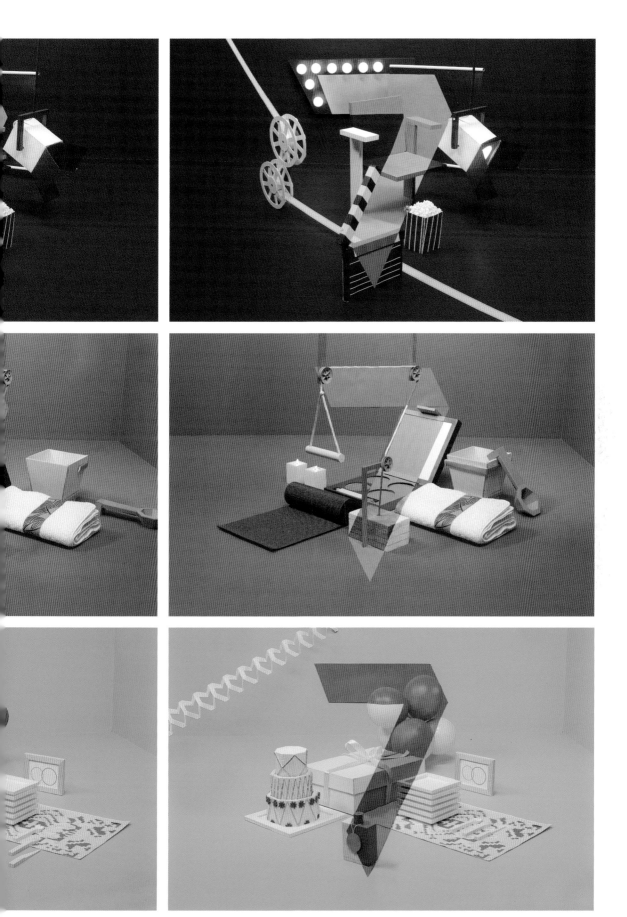

GÖTE-
BORGSTRY-
CKERIET

by **Happy F&B**

The impulsion to blaze a trail in printing is integral to the Swedish printing house which has been in business since 1918. Dressed up totally in refreshing colours, the new identity highlights the century-old printer's technical creativity and desire to experiment with a modernised brand icon. Every item, from labels and business cards to boxes and samples, are delicately produced to inspire creative designs made possible by quality printing.

LOCATION/
Gothenburg, Sweden
NATURE/
Printer

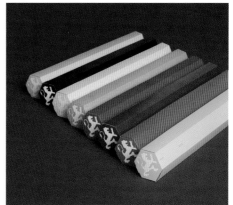

ANORAK

by **Heydays**

Having the company name and everything halved by a line might not be a normal solution for identity design, but Heydays' solution points directly to Anorak's cut-through attitude and agency-client relationship as they develop ad campaigns. The line is used in a number of ways, as tear-off opening in the middle of Anorak's envelopes, tipped edges on business cards, stretchable bands on folders and graphics on the office interior.

LOCATION/
Oslo, Norway
NATURE/
Advertising Consultant

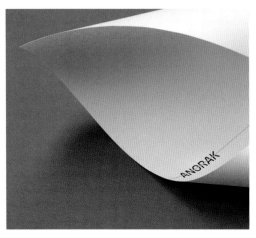

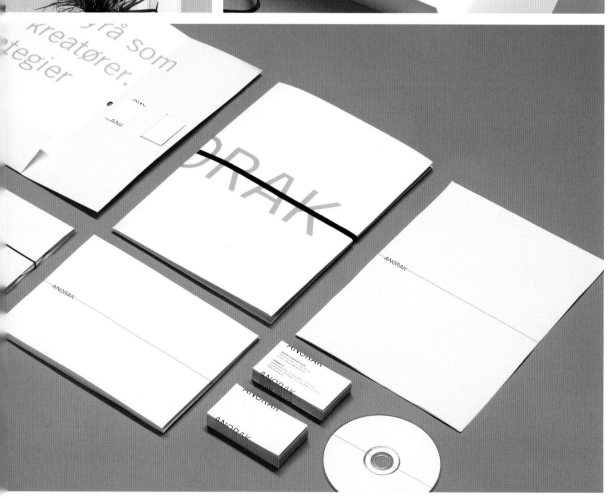

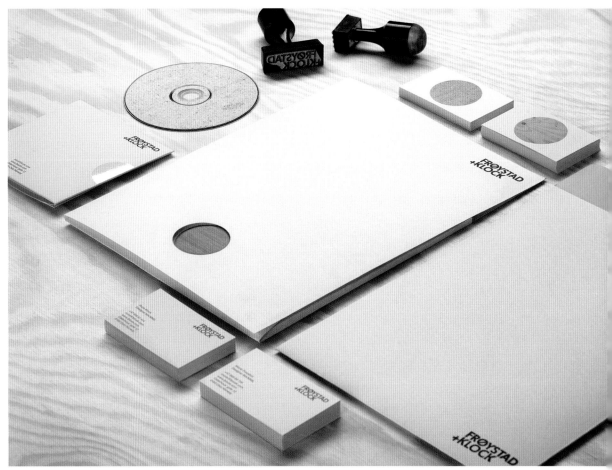

FRØYSTAD
+KLOCK

by **Heydays**

Frøystad+Klock commissioned a light identity to communicate their eyes for details and careful use of materials in their furniture design. Inspired by Scandinavian design traditions, Heydays reduced the concept to a minimal visual combination with focuses on their word-mark. On two sets of colour paper stock separating the partners are 12 distinctive grain and fabric patterns commonly seen in the duo's products. A subtle mention of their partnership is revealed in the DVD sleeve as it unfolds.

LOCATION/
Oslo, Norway
NATURE/
Furniture Design
Partners

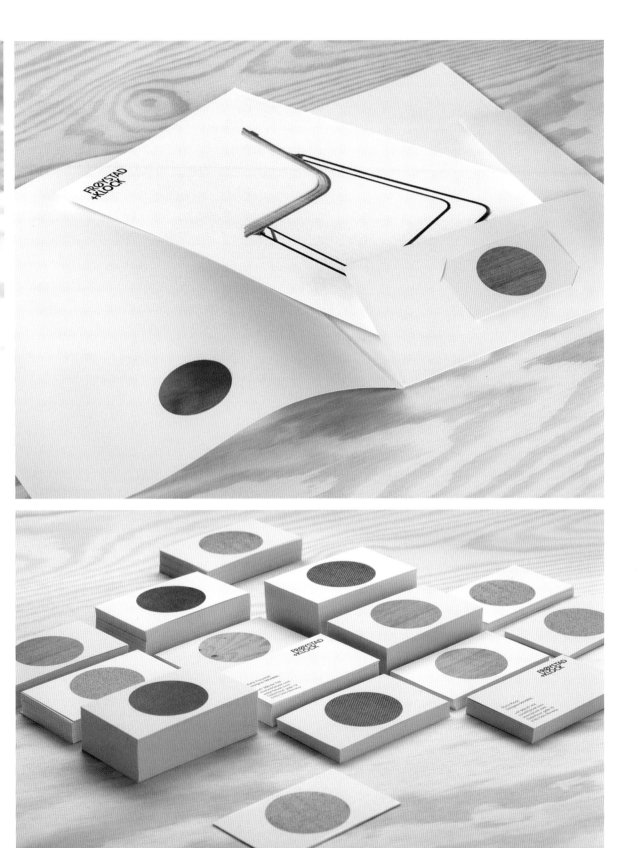

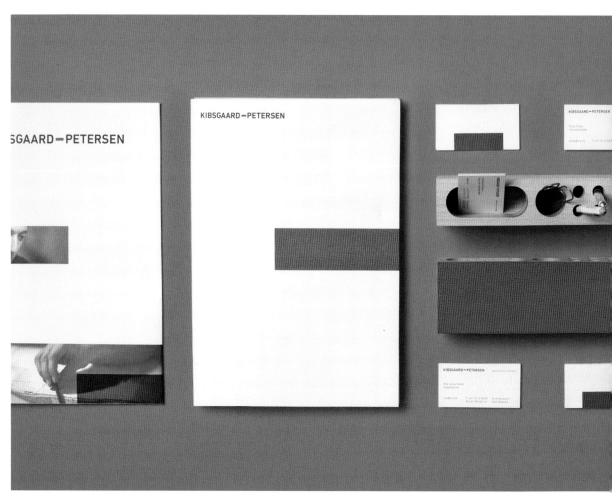

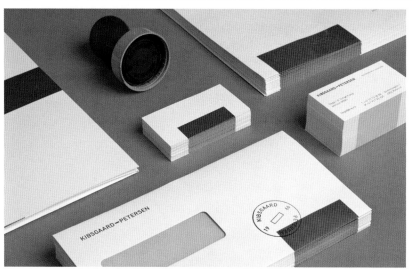

KIBSGAARD–PETERSEN

by **Heydays**

The visions and beliefs of Ola Kibsgaard–Petersen and his namesake architecture practice are all embraced in a red, bold hyphen taken from his name. While the colour and dash form a strong architectural language, the stamping and embossing add to a synergy between young innovation and solid traditions that motivate the firm. A custom pencil holder was also made based on the icon to bring the visual profile into the architects' everyday life.

LOCATION/
Ålesund, Sweden
NATURE/
Architectural Design Firm

11

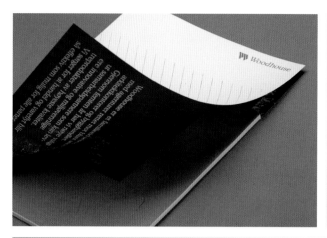

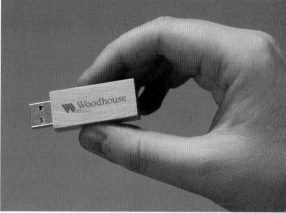

WOODHOUSE

by **Heydays**

The identity of this lumber dealer talks to both its suppliers and clients made of architects and the construction market. An immediate reference with its quality materials and awareness of sustainable development was made through its business cards and prints, with visuals powerfully zooming in on the grain, origins of the wood and timber being processed at different stages. The identity package includes cartons for delivery, USB flash drives, a 3D wood puzzle and tote bags.

LOCATION/
Oslo, Norway
NATURE/
Lumber Dealer

BAUHAUS DESSAU

by **Hort**

Modernism is still at the heart of Bauhaus Dessau Foundation's new identity. But instead of the more expected geometric visual clichés, Courier, considered the most generic and incidental typeface of all was taken to represent the institution as the new corporate font. Alongside strict typography minimalist layout, standardised formats and a natural tone. Arial Black is alternatively employed to play up titles and dates on posters and flyers.

LOCATION/
Dessau, Germany
NATURE/
Academic Foundation

Die neue Linie

19.5. bis 24.8. 2011

DIE NEUE LINIE
DIE MÖBELWERKSTÄTTEN AM BAUHAUS

Ausstellung vom 19.5. bis 24.8.2011
Im Werkstattflügel des Bauhausgebäudes
Geöffnet täglich von 10 bis 18 Uhr
Eintritt: € 8,- / 4,-

Stiftung Bauhaus Dessau
Gropiusallee 38
D-06846 Dessau-Roßlau
www.bauhaus-dessau.de

Kandinsky am Bauhaus

KANDINSKY AM BAUHAUS
WEGE DER ABSTRAKTION

Ausstellung vom 29.1. bis 30.4.2011
Im Werkstattflügel des Bauhausgebäudes
Geöffnet täglich von 10 bis 18 Uhr
Eintritt: € 8,- / 4,-

Stiftung Bauhaus Dessau
Gropiusallee 38
D-06846 Dessau-Roßlau
www.bauhaus-dessau.de

Wege der Abstraktion

29.1. bis 30.4.2011

Architektur und Stadt in der Finanzkrise

Internationale Konferenz
11. bis 14.11.2010

Die neue Linie

19.5. bis 24.8. 2011

Kandinsky am Bauhaus

Wege der Abstraktion

29.1. bis 30.4.2011

Spielplan 2010
Mai bis Dezember

Musik am Bauhaus

Bauhäusler mit der Kamera

Eine Bilderschau

12.5. bis 29.8.2010

BAUHÄUSLER MIT DER KAMERA. EINE BILDERSCHAU

1923 kam der ungarische Maler, Grafiker und Fotograf László Moholy-Nagy ans Bauhaus. Mit ihm seine Kamera, die fortan nicht mehr wegzudenken sein sollte aus dem Leben an der Schule. Plötzlich gab es ein Bild vom Bauhaus, mehr noch, Bilder verschiedenster Form und Machart. Die Bauhäusler nutzten Fotoapparate für künstlerische Experimente, fotografisch dokumentierten sie das Leben an der Schule. Und sie hatten einen Weg entdeckt, um ihre Produkte bekannt zu machen. Die Fotografie beeinflusste das Bild der Hochschule für Gestaltung in der Öffentlichkeit nachhaltig.

Am 11. Mai 2010 um 19 Uhr wird die Schau im Meisterhaus Kandinsky/Klee eröffnet. Bereits vor der Vernissage hat die Presse Gelegenheit zu einem ersten Blick in die Ausstellung. Annemarie Jaeggi, Direktorin des Bauhaus-Archiv Berlin, und Regina Bittner, stellvertretende Direktorin der Stiftung Bauhaus Dessau, führen in einer Pressevorbesichtigung am 11. Mai 2010 um 11 Uhr im Meisterhaus Kandinsky/Klee, Ebertallee 69/71, 06846 Dessau-Roßlau durch die Ausstellung. „Wir freuen uns sehr über die Möglichkeit dieses gemeinsamen Projekts", sagte Philipp Oswalt, Direktor der Stiftung Bauhaus Dessau. Im Vorfeld. „Im fünfzigsten Jahr des Bestehens des Bauhaus-Archiv ist diese Ausstellung ein Signal der Gemeinschaft, sie steht für die produktive gemeinsame Arbeit der Bauhaus-Institutionen in Deutschland."

Öffnungszeiten:
Dienstag bis Sonntag, 10 bis 18 Uhr
Eintritt: € 5,- / 3,-
Meisterhaus Kandinsky/Klee
Ebertallee 69/71
06846 Dessau-Roßlau

Eine Ausstellung des Bauhaus-Archiv Berlin in Kooperation mit der Stadt Dessau-Roßlau und der Stiftung Bauhaus Dessau. Sie ist ab 12. Mai bis 29. August 2010 im Meisterhaus Kandinsky/Klee zu sehen.

EASTFIELD VILLAGE

by **Hovard Design**

To reflect the zeitgeist of the 18th century American trade workshops the historic Eastfield village hosts, as much as possible Hovard developed an identity attainable through the use of production techniques from the period, including antique wood types, letterpress and rubber stamps. The materials used are also a rational choice that celebrates the properties' eclectic nature through a sense of modern simplicity and detailing in designs with a rustic feel.

LOCATION/
New York, US
NATURE/
Cultural Establishments
PHOTO/
Mark Gross

LION IS THE SUN

by **Ivan Khmelevsky**

Moscow-based music agency has been doing a great job at organising shows for indie musicians and bands. But more than picturing this business as entertainment, Ivan Khmelevsky rendered the brand as a synonym of a serious dialogue between artists and audience, a platform for music, other than just party and beers. Aside from the stationery items, the set also comprises a series of merchandise for music lovers to manifest their attitude towards music, so as their support for the agency.

LOCATION/
Moscow, Russia

NATURE/
Music Agency

**SAVIER
KHMELEVSKY**
PROMOTER

+7 926 594–89–40
savier@lionisthesun.com
www.lionisthesun.com

Verhnyaya Pervomayskaya
2/32, 82, Moscow, Russia
105264

LION IS THE SUN

**SAVIER
KHMELEVSKY**
PROMOTER

+7 926 594–89–40
savier@lionisthesun.com
www.lionisthesun.com

Verhnyaya Pervomayskaya
2/32, 82, Moscow, Russia
105264

BOREALIS

by **Jessica Walsh**

Formed in 1976 at the Juilliard School of Music, the five members of Borealis Wind Quintet shared a love of music, friendship and the goal to play the best music with flute, oboe, clarinet, horn and bassoon. For maximum colour and variety like the aurora borealis and their performances, Jessica Walsh proposed a collection of artwork and an custom logotype printed on iridescent foil to present the ensemble on communications, business cards and album covers.

LOCATION/
Pennsylvania, US
NATURE/
Chamber Ensemble

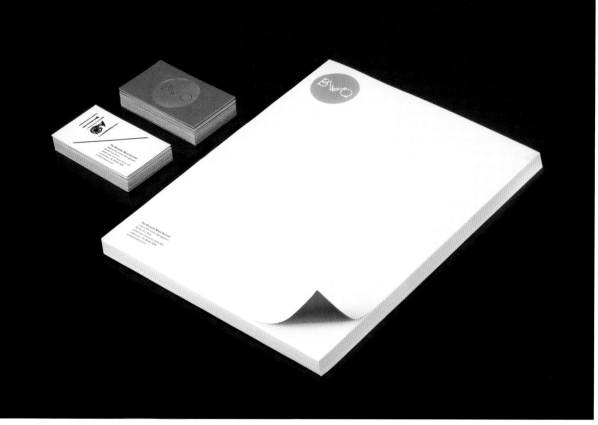

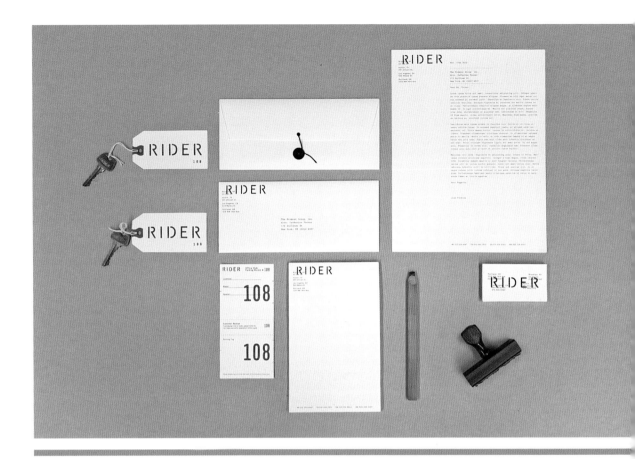

RIDER

----

by **Josh Finklea**

'Rider' is commonly referred as the set of hospitality and technical requests that a band sets as criteria for a performance, and hence the name for the proposed boutique hotel that exclusively caters to touring musicians. Whereas the stencil typeface touches on the iconic road case labelling system, its business cards take on a figurative layout to denote the distribution of the four Rider hotels across the States.

LOCATION/
US
NATURE/
Hotel Chain
CONSULTATION/
Clive Piercy

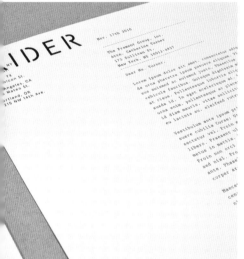

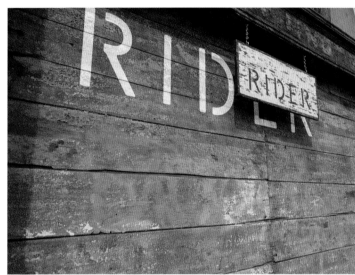

ESTÚDIO VII

by **Juliano Simões da Rocha, Eduardo dos Santos**

Estúdio Vii's corporate stationery exemplifies how environmental and aesthetic creeds can work together. Setting the goal to manifest the most of their qualities with as least environmental impact as possible, the partners stamped and screenprinted every bit of their office supply in house. The hexagonal logo and circulation pattern express their teamwork, commitment to work and systematic approach — like bees.

LOCATION/
Joinville, Brazil
NATURE/
Graphic Design Partners

···ESTÚDIO···

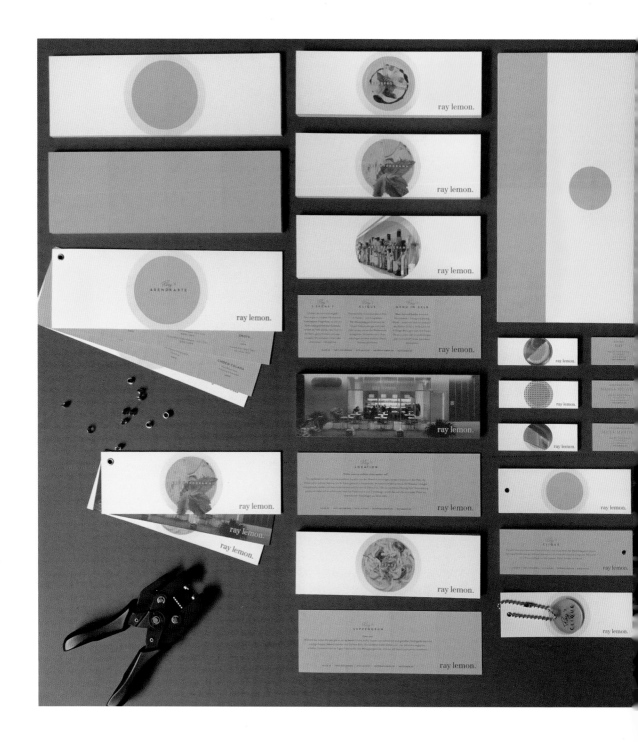

RAY LEMON.

Ray is a friendly, courteous and dedicated (imagined) character who stays in your heart. He represents this bar where anyone can savour delicious food and mingle with people at their monthly events in its fair-faced concrete environment contrasted by lemon yellow. Cohering the brand's frank and cool image, invitations to one of its functions, Menu in Gelb, are manually folded into shape. The featuring spice of the month's menu will also be enveloped as a prelude to perk the recipients up.

by **LSDK**

LOCATION/
Heilbronn, Germany
NATURE/
Casual Dining
Restaurant

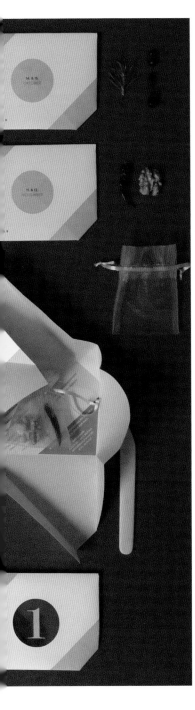

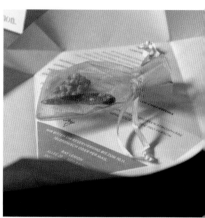

Ray's
LOCATION

en es wirklich schön werden soll?

um den Abend zu verbringen,

ray

ray lem

ray lemon.

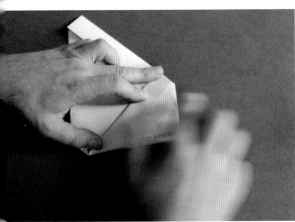

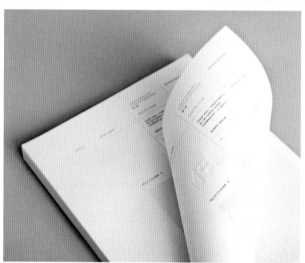

MARU

Lundgren+Lindqvist

Maru is a Japanese boutique setting foot on Oslo street. The story of travelling and the delicacy of its porcelain and handicrafts are communicated in a fusion of elements, combining embossing and debossing, Kanji and English characters and typefaces. Other rational details include dotted graphics that suggest Maru's literal meaning as 'circle' or 'round' in Japanese, coordinating Japanese traditional spot colours and paper stock that embraces the feel of the classic rice paper.

LOCATION/
Fornebu, Norway
NATURE/
Lifestyle Product Retailer
PHOTO/
Kalle Sanner

28 HONG-KONG ST.

by **Manic Design**

28 HongKong Street is a New York-inspired cocktail bar where guests visit for its contemporary social food and a nice good drink. Although its print, packaging and identity work are expected to be touched only by a selected few, much effort is made to communicate its brand positioning between classic and contemporary. The careful curation of materials, typefaces and finish enriches the message with tactility on nearly everything, from matte black embossing to leather coasters.

LOCATION/
Singapore, Singapore
NATURE/
Cocktail Bar

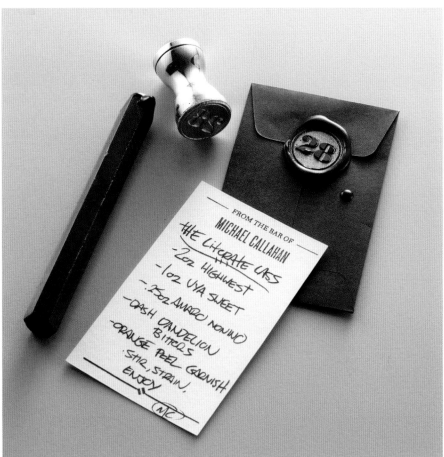

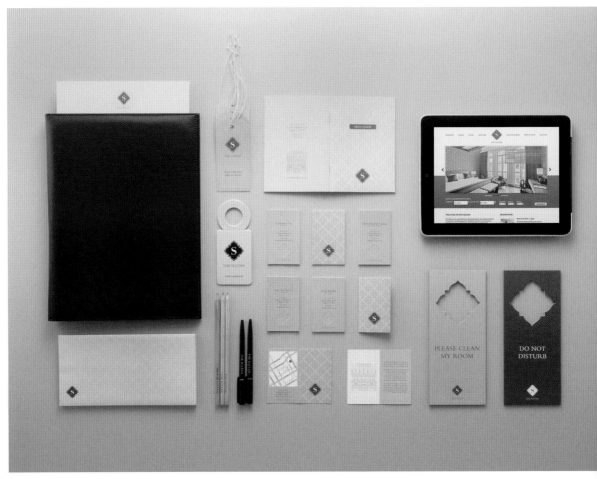

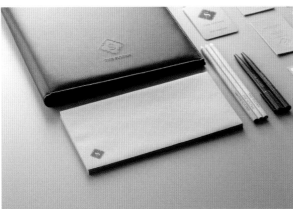

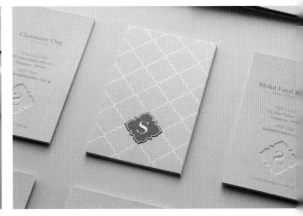

THE SULTAN

by **Manic Design**

Located in Kampong Glam, Singapore, The Sultan is a new boutique hotel converted from ten traditional shophouses, with much of its Arabic architectural features faithfully preserved. The decorative work and ivory palette in the identity is a nod to the area's unique Arabic and Malay roots, with a taste of modern elegance and old-world Singaporean charm. The scope comprises a comprehensive list of corporate and in-room items, as well as a custom area guide for guests.

LOCATION/
Singapore, Singapore
NATURE/
Boutique Hotel

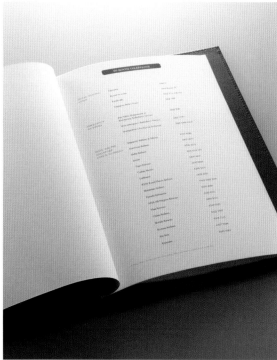

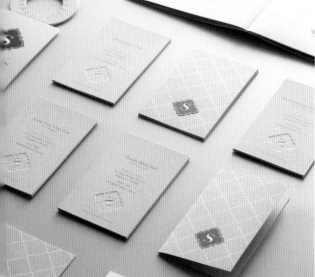

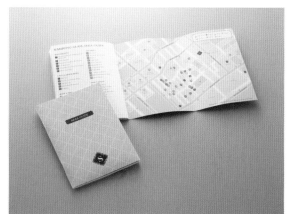

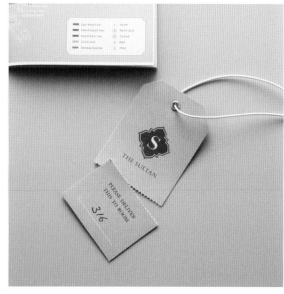

ESTUDIO
TANGUMA

by **Manifiesto Futura**

Taking the interior design firm's name as the starting point, Manifiesto Futura's intent was to put as much visual reference to the native American word as possible in the brand. A mosaic pattern emanating a strong aura of Indian and native American fabric aesthetic was designed to swell the firm's look and roots on every point of touch.

LOCATION/
Mexico
NATURE/
Interior Design Firm

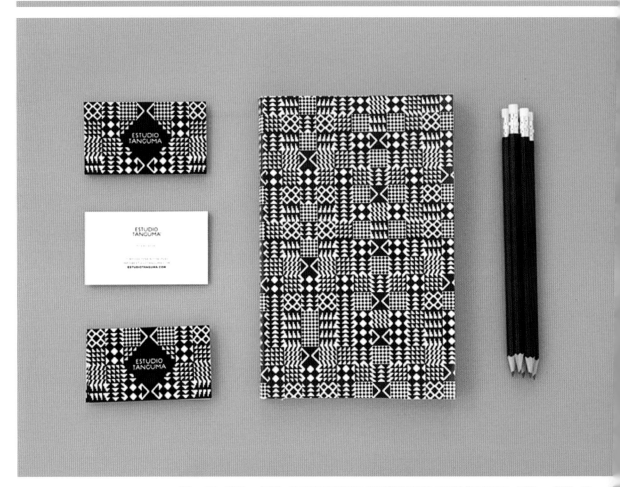

MAMINENA

by **Manifiesto Futura**

Mexican culture is thrilling and unqiue in every way. It is a place of stories, culture and history that can be found no where else in this world. For Maminena, a boutique hotel that welcomes fascinated tourists from around the world, the complex sensation is translated into pictures of the old times and a kaleidoscopic pattern. The recollection is meant to be an alternative channel to open Mexico to anyone who wish to learn the different faces of the beautiful Mexico today.

LOCATION/
Mexico
NATURE/
Boutique Hotel
ARCHITECTURE/
Laboratorios Vaquero

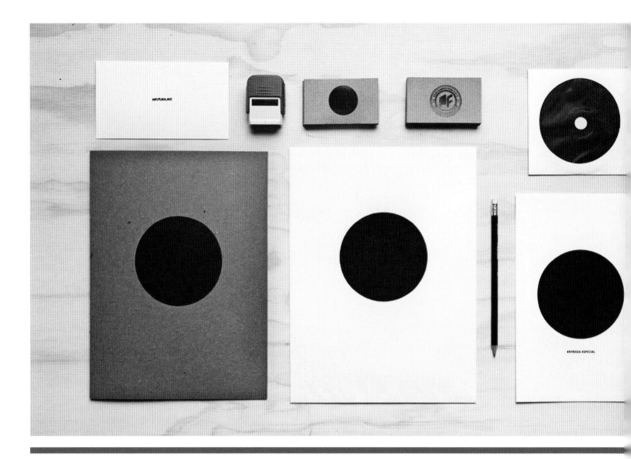

MFUTURA.

by **Manifiesto Futura**

Manifiesto Futura prides themselves on their creative delivery beyond pure graphic solutions. Taking their own identity as a platform to showcase their doctrine, the designers focused their efforts on optimising available resources to build the most practical solution for communications. Besides a typographic emblem, the studio also drew on a full stop to represent their integral approach and leave space for clients to imagine what can be retrieved from inside that dark infinite space.

LOCATION/
Monterrey, Mexico
NATURE/
Graphic Design Studio

NUESTRO
PROCESO DE TRABAJO.

ENTREGA ESPECIAL

THE SLANTED DOOR

by **Manual**

Overlooking San Francisco Bay, The Slanted Door has been Charles Phan's kitchen for modern Vietnamese cuisine since 1995. For a more genuine definition of the restaurant's concept, a clean logotype accentuated with a sloping line was developed to highlight family values and personality traits in Phan's culinary art. The idea of 'slanted' recurs on the restaurant's documents and menus as tilted graphics and angled folds.

LOCATION/
San Francisco, US
NATURE/
Fine Dining Restaurant

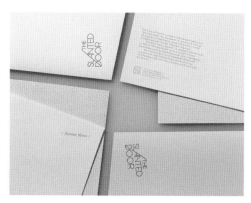

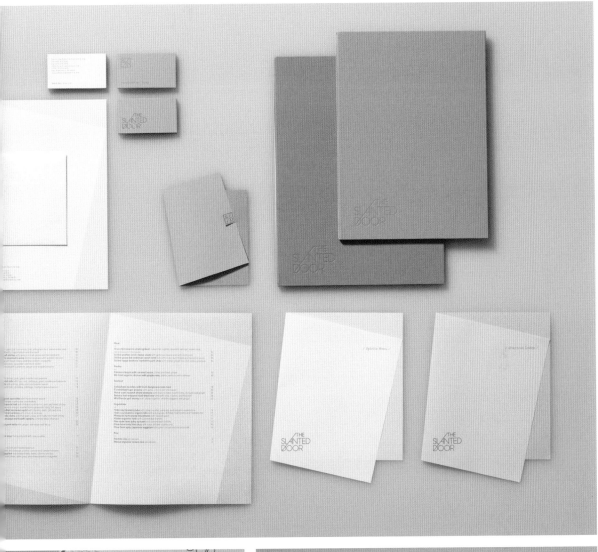
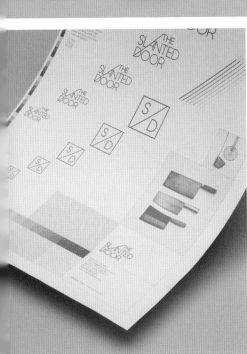
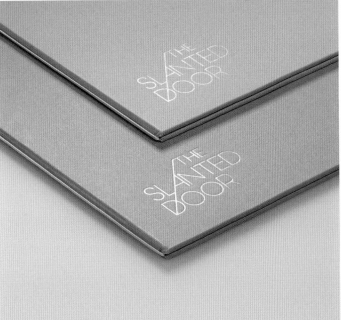

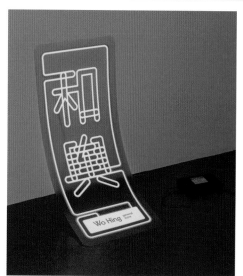

Wo Hing General Store is the owner's homage to his father and uncle who used to run a small grocery store in Vietnam after fleeing China. Visual references to its Chinese street food and crafted cocktail offerings are made through the delicate forms of raw and cooked noodles, imaged as the main staple on the diner's prints. A tube-based Chinese logotype reinforces the identity with blind embossing and electroluminescent ink print on the shop's window sign.

LOCATION/
San Francisco, US
NATURE/
Bar and Restaurant

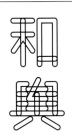

Wo
Hing
general
store

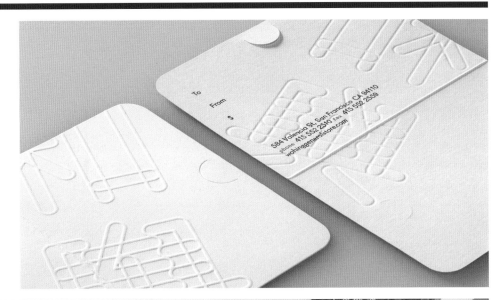

Ā

ALLA HORN

ALLA HORN

Alla Horn interior design house prioritises functionality in their visual solutions. The crucial steps of planning and sketching at the beginning of their creative process are thus accentuated in its logo, featuring a pencil formed by the studio's initials, with an 'A' topping the 'H'. GT Haptik by Grilli, specially optimised to be touched and read blindfolded, was selected to complement the emphases and Alla Horn's approach to design.

by **Marcus Hollands**

LOCATION/
Brisbane, Australia
NATURE/
Interior Design Firm

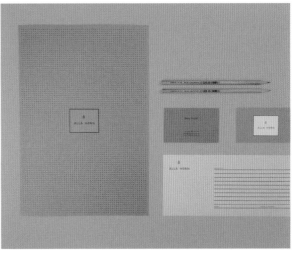

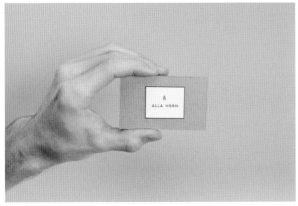

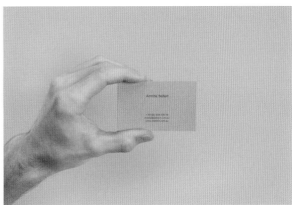

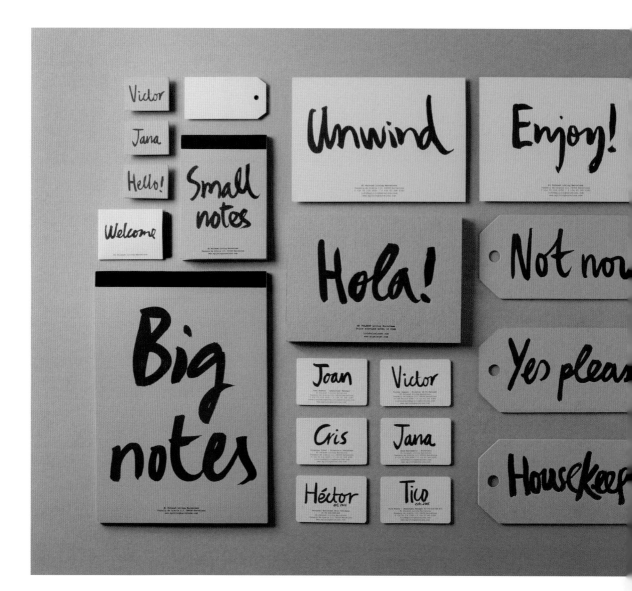

EL PALAUET
LIVING
BARCELONA

by **Marnich Associates**

With a vision to offer new city living in the capital city of Spain, El Palauet Living Barcelona housed in a listed modernista building communicates sophistication in a posh red hand-lettering against an off-white background that runs all the way from period ceilings to modern fixtures. Mixed printing technique, such as foil stamping, screen-printing and embossing, are employed on recycled papers and cardboard to elevate the minimal design in tune with their advocacy of sustainability.

LOCATION/
Barcelona, Spain
NATURE/
Serviced Apartment
LETTERING/
Pol Montserrat

1

El Palauet Living Barcelona

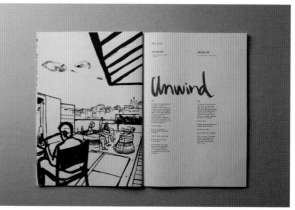

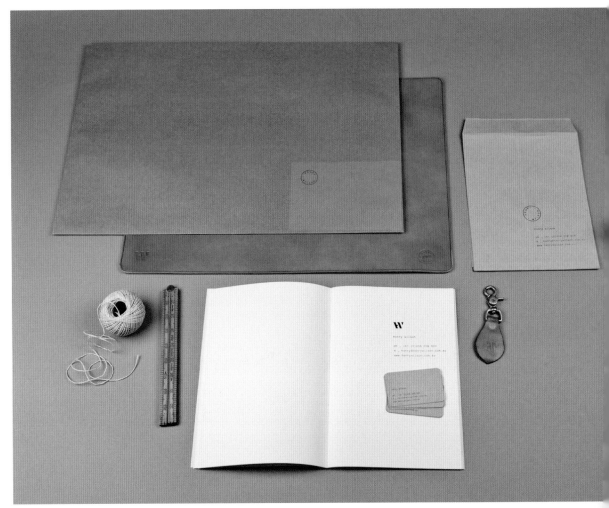

HENRY WILSON

by **Maud**

Henry Wilson's strong belief in design as a response to real needs guided Maud's approach deliverable with a couple of stamps. While Wilson's lighting fixtures and fittings make a personal statement in their utilitarian nature and crafted forms, so does his brandmark appearing bright and distinctive wherever it is applied or impressed. The young Australian designer is presented by two marks, with his initials and full name, that work individually and as one.

LOCATION/
Sydney, Australia
NATURE/
Independent Product
Designer

henry wilson

ph - +61 (0)408 209 600
e - henry@henrywilson.com.au
www.henrywilson.com.au

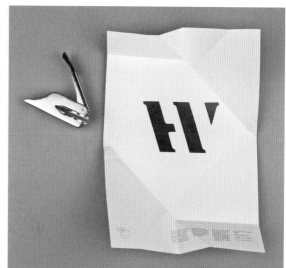

MEANWHILE

by **Maud**

Meanwhile is a new menswear boutique located in the exclusive Kings Cross Hills of Sydney, where the finest Australian labels are stocked alongside international greats. Making it cost effective and low maintenance whilst retaining the considered craftsmanship that the shop represents, Maud created an identity using only inked hand stamps. The brandmark itself is the joining of an 'M' and a 'W' that alludes to a tailor's stitch.

LOCATION/
New South Wales, Australia
NATURE/
Menswear Boutique

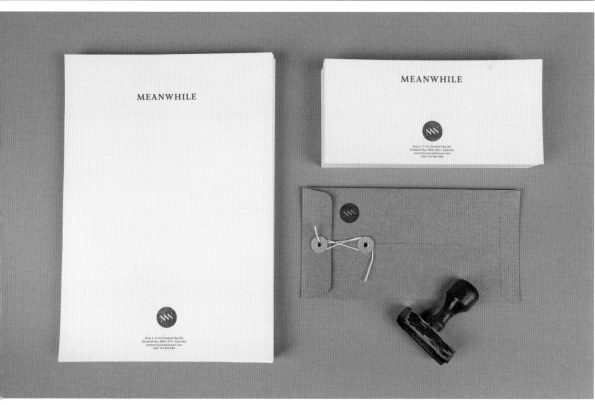

DIVISION
OF LABOR

by **Mikey Burton**

Creative and strategic brand studio, Division of Labor, wanted a light-hearted brand image which "no one would confuse with an actual government agency". The partners' business cards were a modernised edition of the union membership card where every piece of information is letterpressed on French Poptone. The studio's logo specifies their areas of expertise in four graphic icons, with a line of Latin remarks saying 'Don't let the bastards grind you down'.

LOCATION/
San Francisco, US
NATURE/
Strategic Branding Firm
ART DIRECTION/
Josh Denberg,
Paul Hirsch

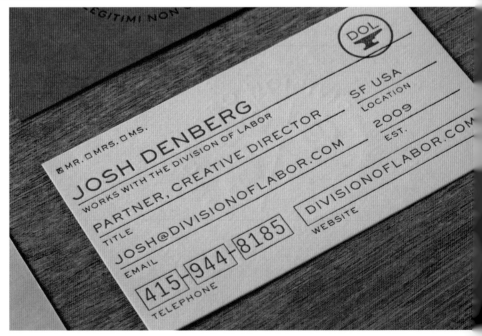

MAREINER
HOLZ

by **moodley brand identity**

Mareiner Holz believes in natural beauty. For this reason, the Austrian crafter has developed a whole range of plank finishing that is practical, environmentally friendly and best to reserve the unique features for all kinds of wood. The stylised woodpecker trademarks Holz's agility and obstinacy. For typeface, Gotham was chosen to accent the logo for its geometric form and the classic Garamond Pro to reinforce the brand's bond with nature in the competent line.

LOCATION/
Sankt Marein im Mürztal
Austria
NATURE/
Wood Finishing Firm

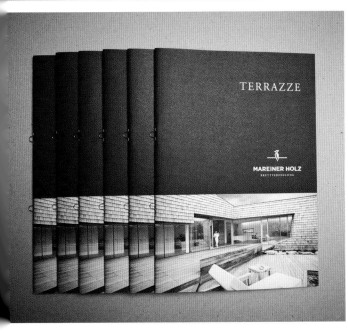

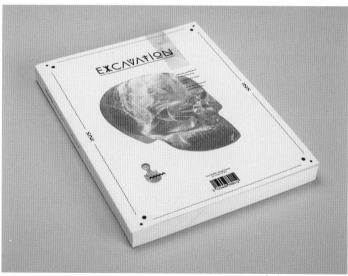

EXCAVATION

(Fictional) archeology museum, Excavation, has numerous channels to prepare its visitors to travel back time and walk into the eminent world of artefacts spanning themes of death, religion and warfare. Visible on its entry tickets, business cards, programmes and publications, the flickering graphics and bespoke typeface were designed to allude to the eclectic nature of ancient cultures with a relatively symbolic approach in textual form.

NATURE/
Cultural Institution

by **Morey Talmor**

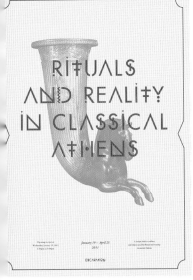

RITUALS AND REALITY IN CLASSICAL ATHENS

DEATH ON DISPLAY IN THE ANCIENT WORLD

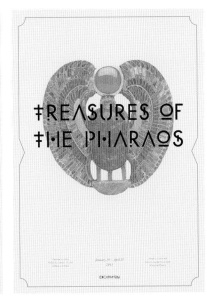

TREASURES OF THE PHARAOS

NOEEKO

by **Noeeko**

Noeeko is the brainchild of Polish art director and graphic designer Michael Sycz. Open to creations in a board range of media, Sycz chose to draw client's attention back to his freelance name and brand his communication items with a logomark combining 'E' and 'K' of its name. The colour scheme runs all the way from prints to his official website for a coordinated look.

LOCATION/
Warsaw, Poland
NATURE/
Independent Graphic
Designer

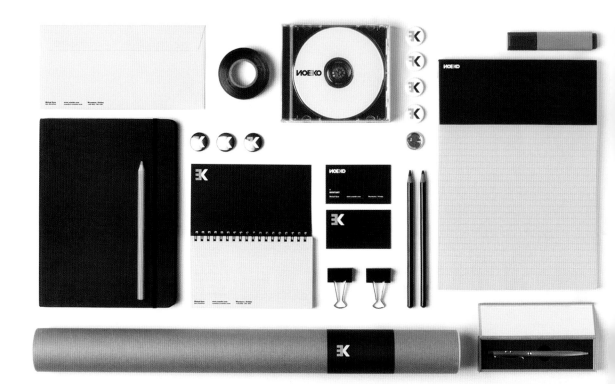

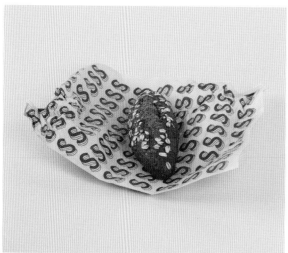

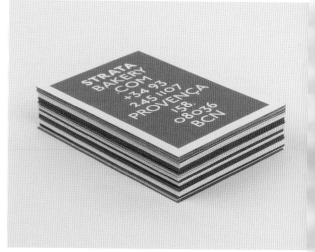

STRATA
BAKERY

by **P•A•R**

The countless layers of ingredients in their homemade cakes has given the bakery its signature recipe and name. Starting with this concept, P•A•R designed a graphic synthesis of Strata's pastry and cakes with a striking chromatic range, most obvious when the promotional boards are stacked up and notepads are closed. The identity package also includes wrappers and stickers featuring the bakery's name in triple layers.

LOCATION/
Barcelona, Spain
NATURE/
Bakery

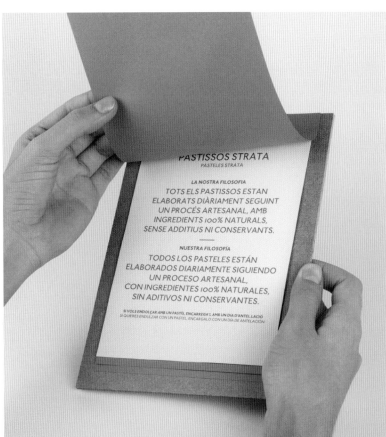

PASTISSOS STRATA
PASTELES STRATA

LA NOSTRA FILOSOFIA
TOTS ELS PASTISSOS ESTAN
ELABORATS DIÀRIAMENT SEGUINT
UN PROCÉS ARTESANAL, AMB
INGREDIENTS 100% NATURALS,
SENSE ADDITIUS NI CONSERVANTS.

NUESTRA FILOSOFÍA
TODOS LOS PASTELES ESTÁN
ELABORADOS DIARIAMENTE SIGUIENDO
UN PROCESO ARTESANAL,
CON INGREDIENTES 100% NATURALES,
SIN ADITIVOS NI CONSERVANTES.

SI VOLS ENDOLÇAR AMB UN PASTÍS, ENCARREGA'L AMB UN DIA D'ANTEL·LACIÓ
SI QUIERES ENDULZAR CON UN PASTEL, ENCÁRGALO CON UN DÍA DE ANTELACIÓN

SOMMELIER
MARKOV
ANATOLY

by **Pavel Emelyanov**

The personal identity of Russian sommelier Markov Anatoly comes as a case-organiser kit. Like a proper wine carton, aptly inscribed with monograms, quantity and volume of bottles contained and an IPPC mark, etc., the case also holds a variety of tools for the sommelier to manufacture business cards with remarks on the date of manufacturing or wine opening.

LOCATION/
Murmansk, Russia
NATURE/
Sommelier
PHOTO/
Pleshkov Andrey

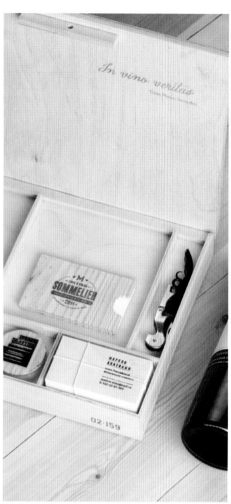

ADAM
AND EVE

by **Raewyn Brandon**

Formed by creative professionals who share the legal knowledge and commitment to intellectual property, Adam and Eve conceived a rather unorthodox take on identity, using the frame of the Ten Commandments to hit on its accidental relevance to the biblical characters, so as to identify their ten beliefs. The eco-friendly materials are a note on the firm's dedication to environmental protection.

LOCATION/
Hamilton, New Zealand
NATURE/
Legal Advisor

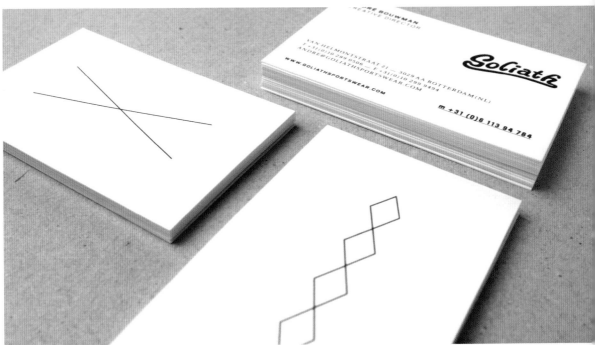

GOLIATH
SPORTSWEAR

by **Studio Beige**

Eighty-five years ago, a shoemaker's son created a footwear brand for people passionate about details; 85 years later, they continue their devotion to details within an enlivened outward look to speak its classic chic. Without forgoing the brand's traditions and beliefs, Studio Beige created a visual world that articulate Goliath's values in its most classic text forms. The identity can also be recognised on print communications tailored for its brand communities worldwide.

LOCATION/
Rotterdam,
the Netherlands
NATURE/
Sportswear
Manufacturer

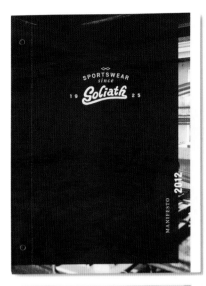

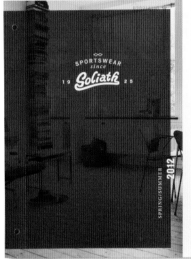

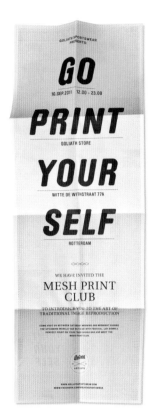

KCR

by **Studio Beige**

Kenniscentrum Cultuureducatie Rotterdam is an independent body set up to help educational institutions select and develop art programmes that best fit their goals. Looking for a simple element to depict KCR's versatility, Studio Beige came up with a design based on right triangles, configured in various shades of green. The element recurs in the body of tilings, graphics and snips that appear different yet coordinated as one.

LOCATION/
Rotterdam,
the Netherlands
NATURE/
Cultural Institution

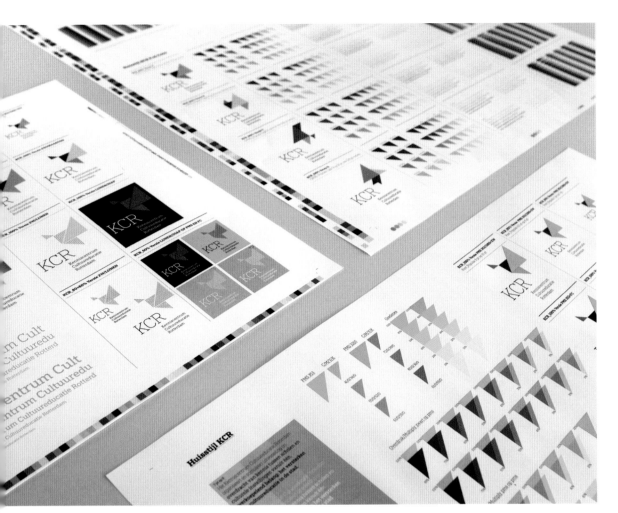

KCR
versterkt
cultuureducatie

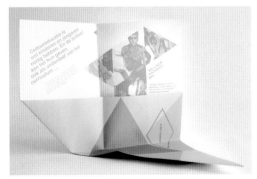

STUDIO
BEIGE

by **Studio Beige**

Dutch design studio Studio Beige cherishes a love for typography and clarity in whichever print matters and web design they do. The studio's own identity is no exception. But instead of a pale sandy colour, they opted for a bright yellow to glow on the edge and back of their communication tools. Greetings like "Nice to meet you" and "See you soon" are blind-embossed on their business cards and invitations as a tactile surprise for the recipients.

LOCATION/
Rotterdam,
the Netherlands
NATURE/
Graphic Design Studio

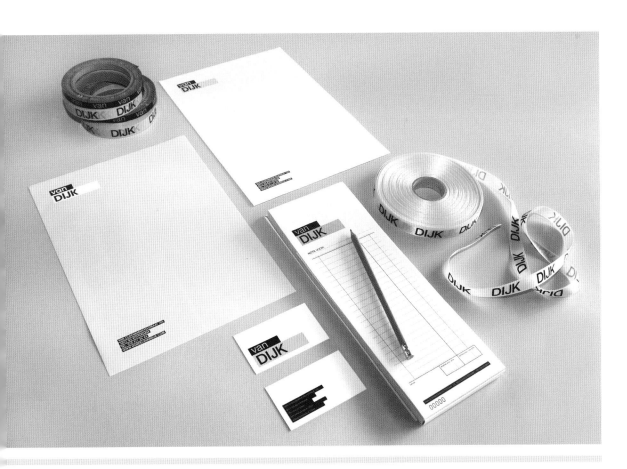

VANDIJK

by **Studio Beige**

Situated at the heart of Rotterdam, vanDIJK is the place for fine cashmere knits, jogging trousers, classic pumps, dresses and suits by exclusive brands. Advocating a new fashion charisma that blends femininity with androgyny, the boutique's vision is translated into graceful pink and neutral black. The colours exchange as they highlight the shop's name on ribbons, invoice and as letterheads.

LOCATION/
Rotterdam,
the Netherlands
NATURE/
Fashion Boutique

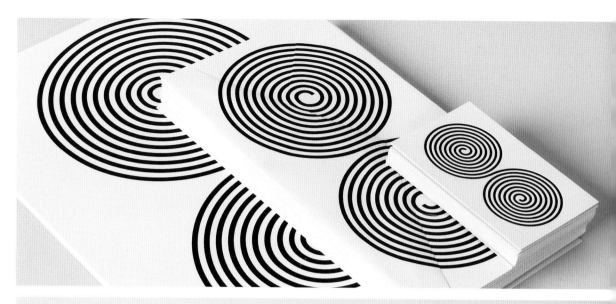

STAMPA

by **Studio Lin**

Stampa does not only stimulate optical senses with its exclusive archival prints, but also its logo mark depicting an 'S' as two jumbo reels. The logomark was drawn in six sizes to retain the optical vibration wherever it is needed to be used. A custom typeface was commissioned throughout Stampa's print stationery and online pieces to further distinguish the brand.

LOCATION/
New York, US
NATURE/
E-commerce Portal
LETTERING/
Benjamin Critton

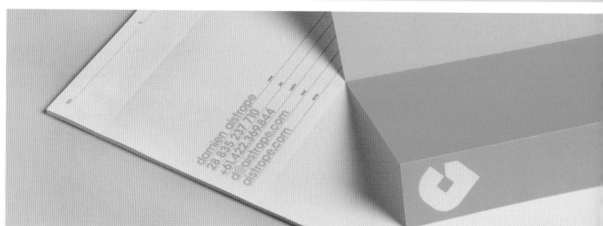

AISTROPE

by **Studio Verse**

Commissioned to develop a bold typographic identity and stationery to complement web designer and developer, Damien Aistrope's pre-existing marque, Studio Verse advocated turquoise green and a mixed type setting, with Avant Garde Bold and DIN, to separate information and index. The identity has been clear foiled into triplexed business cards, while the letterhead is perforated to be used as tear-off compliment slips.

LOCATION/
Sydney, Australia
NATURE/
Website Developer

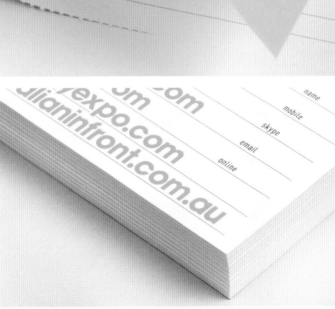

ZANN ST PIERRE

by **Studio Verse**

Identity for web designer Zann St Pierre is based on a two-dimensional marque with a sense of depth. Appearing like a twisted band, the character reflects the amount of effort that goes beyond the surface, into the back-end of coding and developing. Paired with typeface Replica Mono, the design was partially letterpressed on the back of his letters and clear foiled on the front and back of his duplexed business cards to stress the layers of his work.

LOCATION/
Melbourne, Australia
NATURE/
Independent Website Designer

Zann St Pierre
web design/development
mobile no 0405 594 595
skype u/n zannstpierre
email mail@zannstpierre
online www.zann.com.au

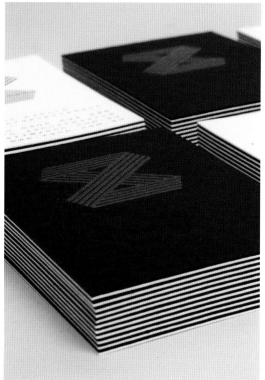

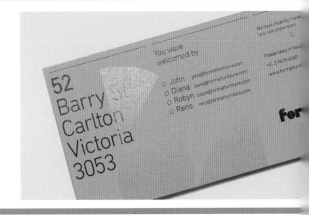

FORMAT
FURNITURE

by **Studio Worldwide**

Format Furniture has asked for an update on their brand identity as they moved to a new address. Highlighting the painted concrete that characterises their new warehouse, Format's new business card-cum-welcome cards came with a thin screenprint over grey cardboard. Varnished shapes extracted from its logotype added another layer to the cards' texture and meaning, indicating mobility, as they shifted over the grids.

LOCATION/
Melbourne, Australia
NATURE/
Furniture Manufactur

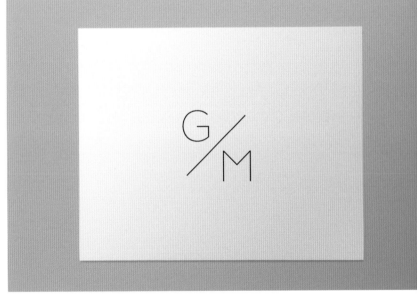

GEORGINA
MATHERSON

by **Studio Worldwide**

G/M is artist-slash-photographer Georgina Matherson who wished to dabble in commercial photography. Direct association with her artistic direction was made through a simple 'slash' drawn from the vocabulary of printmaking, turning each of her notes and business cards into unique numbered prints. Every stationery item, including the perforated business card book, is pressed with a few lines for Matherson to leave a personal note.

LOCATION/
Melbourne, Australia
NATURE/
Independent
Photographer

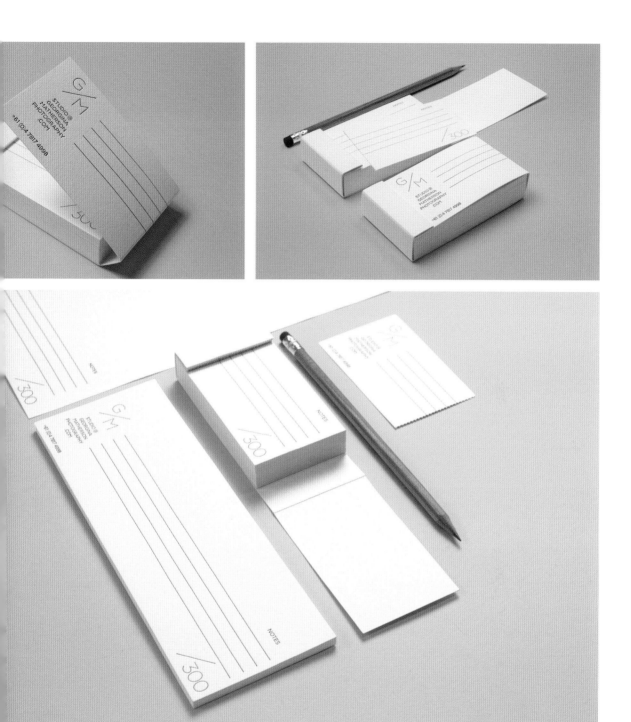

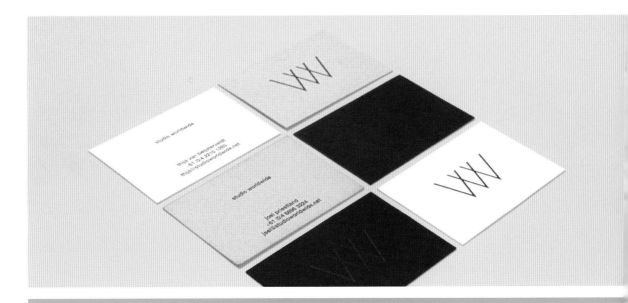

SWW

by **Studio Worldwide**

Studio Worldwide has made a point in their self-promotional items — one of the best things about running a design studio is that whenever you need to restock your stationery, it makes a good chance to explore formats, colours, printing and bold typography. More impulsively, the partners at SWW took a few snapshots from their phones at press checks for their comp cards.

LOCATION/
Melbourne, Australia
NATURE/
Graphic Design Studio

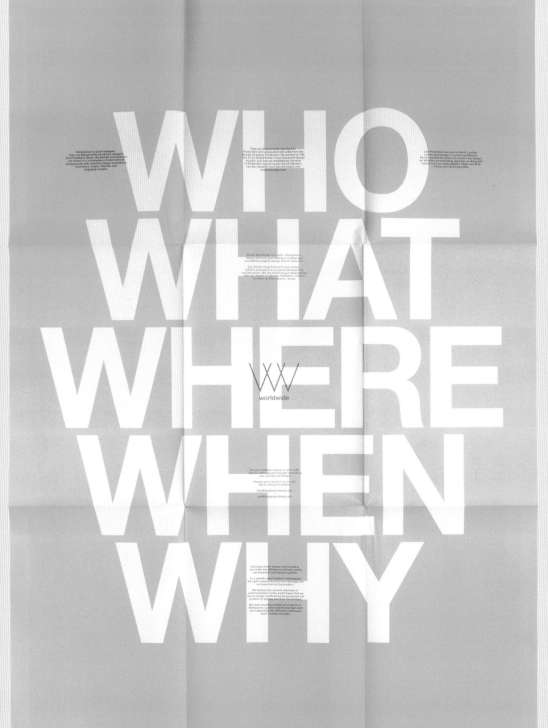

STACK
ARCHITECTS
by **The Consult**

The Consult was delegated to brand Leeds-based architect Robert Bumby's new practice from its name and logo to its identity applications. With a notion to pick out its artistry and as a nod to everyone's earliest experience of building, 'STACK' was picked as the name. The idea was further visualised in three bold blocks and a vertical logotype, with the name broken into separate lines.

LOCATION/
Leeds, UK
NATURE/
Architectural
Design Firm

Stack Architects
Black Building
2 Newton Road
Leeds LS7 4HE

telephone 0113 262 2700
studio@stackarchitects.com
www.stackarchitects.com

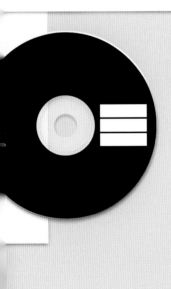

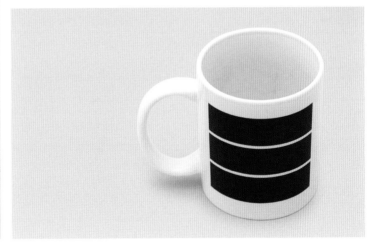

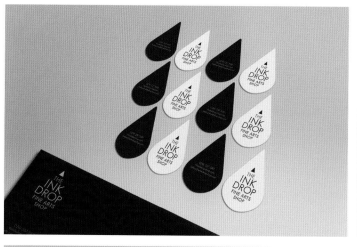

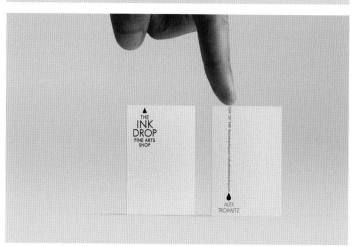

INKDROP

Using an ink drop to symbolise a fine arts shop and its product range comprised of art supplies and inks appears to be a logical solution that appeals to all. For a stronger impression, the ink drop was configured to be recognised in a variety of simple forms. Whether it comes as an invisible outline for its name, physical business cards or just an authentic graphic element, the drop and the shop go in pairs thereafter.

by **Timur Salikhov**

NATURE/
Arts Supplies Shop

JACU

by **Tom Emil Olsen**

Jacu Coffee Roastery is like the famous Jacu bird, with an innate capacity to pick only the best beans from great plantations to roast. While its name makes a direct connection to its product's quality, the entire concept was further reinforced in a graphic typeface inspired by the bird and the beans. The Jacu bird takes a variety of appearance — ink stamps, blind imprints, wax seal and diecuts — on kraft paper to suggest a no-frills quality.

LOCATION/
Ålesund, Norway
NATURE/
Roastery & Café

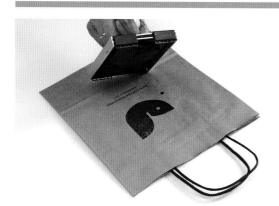

BEYOND
STATIONERY

Branding begins with a clear objective and keeps alive by logical and strategic decisions. From visual elements to management style, it has to balance business ambitions with target customers' needs, impart the ideas in layers and finish with a personality that truly defines the company and connects with whom they want to serve. No doubt, everyone is a unique entity. No single setting can be good enough for all.

· SAN PEDRO GG ·

SOFIA

No. 440

BY PELLI CLARKE PELLI ARCHITECTS

Residencias
&
Suites Corporativas

SOFIA

San Pedro, Mexico
Design • Anagrama
Typeface • SOFIA Sans Display
Paper • Patriot Blue Classic Linen, Natural White Sundance Felt,
Avorio Fabria, Classic Natural Classic Crest

SAN PEDRO GG

DESDE   MMXIII

"ALL ITEMS WILL HAVE TO FUNCTION PERFECTLY AS SELLING TOOLS. WE WORKED REALLY HARD TO FINISH IT AND NOW WE FEEL LIKE WINNING A GAME."

SOFIA is a residential building designed by
Pelli Clarke Pelli Architects led by renowned architect
César Pelli. Located in San Pedro, Mexico, facing the
Valle del Campestre, this building redefines the concept of
modern living with the most generous specifications in
every aspect, from its unique amenities to its world-class
architecture and LEED certified design.

TASK

SOFIA enjoys the advantages of situating in the suburb, with easy access to and the best views of San Pedro, known as the model city of Mexico. Surrounded by nature, SOFIA answers contemporary needs with an integrated package of tranquility, recreation facilities, modern conveniences and world-class architecture in the city.

Our task was to communicate such sophistication and exclusiveness to SOFIA's potential buyers at property sales. Our client, One Development Group, who developed the estate, has insisted on a 'timeless' quality to the branding, that is embedded in the architecture and concept from the start.

CONCEPTION

All items will have to function perfectly as selling tools. They will need to embrace the consistency between the architecture, the living concept and buyers' aspiration to living in style.

We suggested lots of things but the principle idea was to work up the idea in the details, including a good choice of typefaces, paper stock and printing effects. We also proposed to make the name visually more appealing by extending its length. Repeating the house number in the name would be a sensible solution with its direct reference to the building's location.

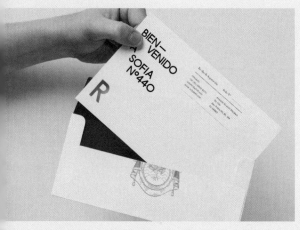

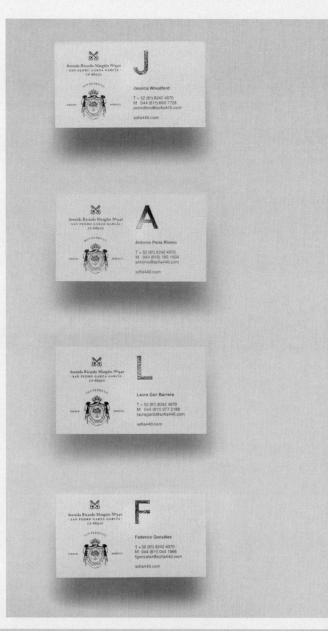

SOLUTION

SOFIA's identity is formed by three very important axes — the keys and the coat of arms inspired by San Pedro's coat of arms; Sofia Sans, a typeface we specially developed for SOFIA based around British san serifs; and the text and information arrangements inspired by the typographic treatment used before grids were popularised by the Swiss grid system.

The developer's high standards for the building's design and attention to needs are delicately translated into the substantial identity package and merchandise. Covering internal operational essentials to informative prospects and giveaways, the branding concept is united with the campaign's stationery, business cards, letterhead, envelopes, email signage, invoice, logo system, sales peripherals, website, print advertisements, location advertisements, signage and brand activation activities.

Five paper stock, each distinct in texture, was chosen to execute the design, with colours comprised of deep blue, off-white and a bright summer plum for accents. Printing techniques include offseting, foil blocking and letterpress.

CASA
SOFIA

COCTEL
BIENVENIDA
ARQ. CESAR PELLI

SOFIA

SO—
FIA

AROMA
SOFIA

SOFIA

SOFIA

BIEN—
VENIDO
A
SO
N°

BIEN—
VENIDO
A
SOFIA
N°440

R

R

EXTRAVAGANZA

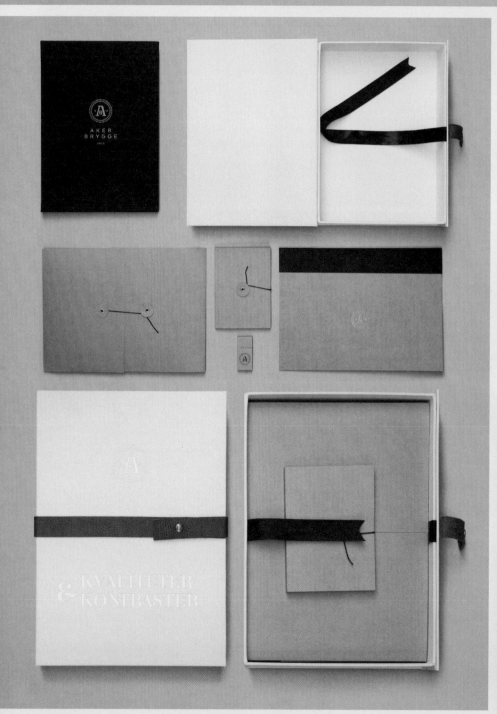

AKER
BRYGGE

OSLO

AKER BRYGGE

Oslo, Norway
Design • Bleed
Photo • Andreas Kleiberg
Typeface • Ellmer Stefan
Paper • Brown board, Scandia 2000, Munken Pure

"WE BELIEVE THE NEW VISUAL IDENTITY SHOULD LIFT THE BRAND OUT OF ITS CURRENT IMAGE, AND TAKE IT TO BECOME AN INCLUSIVE, DIVERSE AND WARM DISTRICT WHERE THE NEW MEETS THE OLD."

Aker Brygge is a commercial district consisted of a shopping centre, offices, residential apartments, bars and restaurants sitting on the harbour of Oslo, Norway. Aker Brygge receives 12 million visitors per year, mostly the highest-earning executives among other tourists and shopping enthusiasts. One of the buildings dates back to 1854 and the entire area was until the early 1980s a mechanical wharf.

TASK

Norwegian Property, the owner of Aker Brygge, commissioned t
identity package as part of their ambitious project to revitalise a
reposition the area both physically and branding-wise. The challen
was for the new identity to bring back some of the industrial past a
incorporate quality, handicrafts and contrasts.

We believe the new visual identity should lift the brand out of its cu
rent image as a cold and modern shopping centre, and take it to b
come an inclusive, diverse and warm district where the new meets t
old and whereby high quality is always evident.

CONCEPTION

With a work group composed of architects, lighting experts and lan
scape architects, Bleed developed an overall brand approach.
re-designed the visual identity to strengthen the district's core valu
and desired brand positioning and rolled it out across a number
applications, ranging from stationery and collateral to signage a
merchandise. The commission also involved art direction in photo
raphy and the design of various print productions, including the 20
page prospectus.

Starting point was at the new architectural drawings, a brand analy
report on the existing brand and an unusually ambitious and vision
brief from the client. The concept was inspired by the physical need
light in this area and the identity is very much linked to Aker Brygg
history and all its contrasts. Similar commercial areas in cities arou
the world were researched.

At the end, we recommended a visual strategy and a mapping of
the branding needs throughout the building process until final co
pletion in 2015.

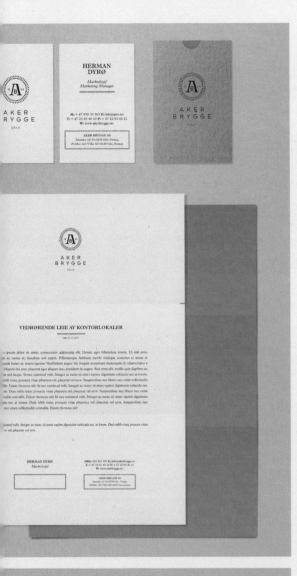

SOLUTION

The greatest challenge was to develop an identity that expresses high-end qualities without being unwelcoming and, at the same time, the appeal for family outings on the harbour as well as high net worth individuals, who work and live on site.

The palette adopted is based on the soft lighting and mood that one can only perceive by the sea at any time of the year within the Aker Brygge area. Aged red, matched with a contrasting green, winter blue with yellow and black are the main colours, however the materials and structure also form a big part of the identity. Taking ownership to cardboard, cotton and paper supports the brand strategy.

The 'sun' in the logo references the light or sun and the industrial history. The custom typeface has its base in history, but also a contemporary angle with ligatures. Materials and colours are not typical for the time. Great attention has been paid on every level of details, such as the colours to adopt on the shopping bag's interior and the patterns to appear on the opening page and end paper of its corporate publications and contracts. The craft conceives its signature through the application of different materials.

With these elements, the client will be able to produce a rich number of coordinating items to boost brand loyalty as the target patrons use their webpage, shopping bags, wrapping paper, etc. round the year.

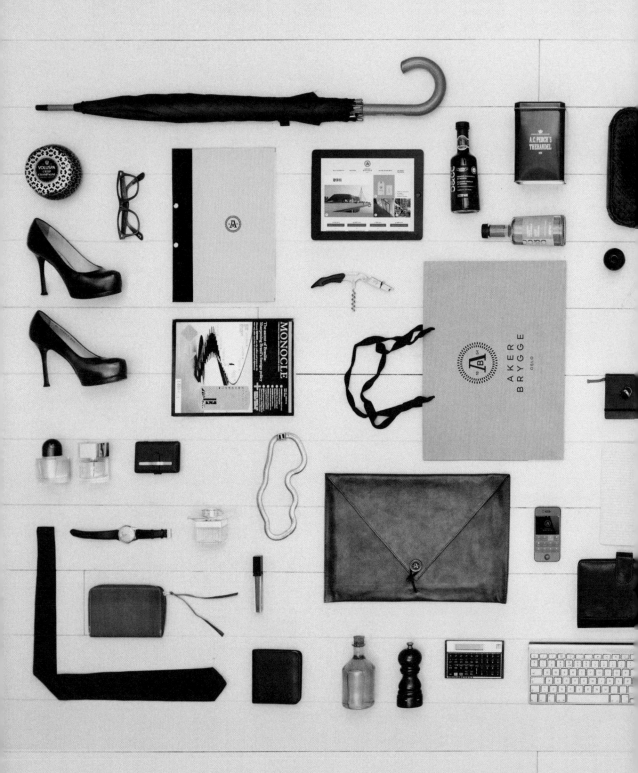

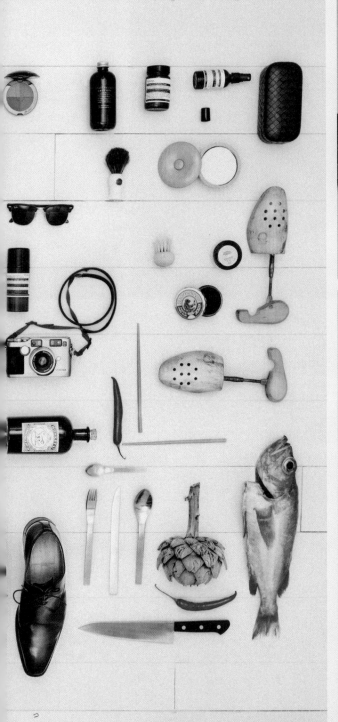

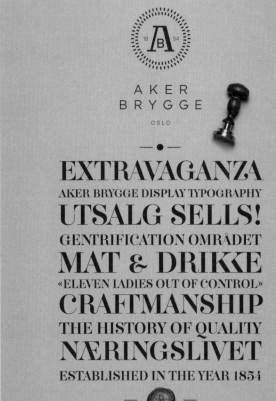

AKER
BRYGGE

OSLO

· • ·

EXTRAVAGANZA
AKER BRYGGE DISPLAY TYPOGRAPHY
UTSALG SELLS!
GENTRIFICATION OMRÅDET
MAT & DRIKKE
«ELEVEN LADIES OUT OF CONTROL»
CRAFTMANSHIP
THE HISTORY OF QUALITY
NÆRINGSLIVET
ESTABLISHED IN THE YEAR 1854

— · —

E. M. SEEFELD

AUSTRIA

MEIER SEEFELD

Seefeld, Austria
Design • Bureau Rabensteiner
Typeface • AT Sackers Gothic, AT Burin
Paper • Curious Skin black, Curious Touch Arches white

meier

SEEFELD

"OUR GOAL WAS TO CREATE AN IDENTITY THAT TRULY RESONATES WITH THE TRADITION AND PEOPLE OF SEEFELD BECAUSE THIS PLACE SHOULD NOT BE JUST 'AN-OTHER' FASHION STORE."

Used to be "La Boutique", Meier is Ernst Meier's fashion boutique based in Seefeld, Austria. His desire for change was triggered by an opportunity to relocate his shop to town square, the most frequented spot in the village. Not knowing what to expect, the entrepreneur thought it was the perfect time for a brand refresh.

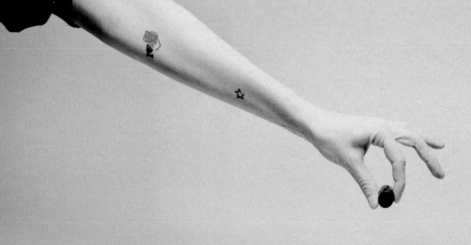

TASK

rnst Meier was already familiar with the work and style of Bureau
abensteiner, which led him to give us the necessary freedom to com-
letely rethink the shop's brand strategy and visualisation. He was a
ery trusting client with a rather loose briefing and thus offered space
r exploration and unique applications.

CONCEPTION

rnst Meier is seen as an institution among the inhabitants of his
ometown, Seefeld. Living and working in the village as a trader his
hole life, Ernst has already grown into a strong brand for himself.

ur goal was to create an identity that truly resonates with the tra-
tion and people of Seefeld. We wanted to leverage this fact and
ange the overall image of the 80s-styled fashion store he has been
nning for years under the name "La Boutique", because this place
ould not be just "another" fashion store but a destination for both
ests and locals.

ur first suggestion was to change the name "La Boutique" to "Meier",
nst's surname. This point was the most crucial in the project devel-
ment and built the core of our concept upon which all other deci-
ns were based.

e design was inspired by the world of skiing and mountaineering
gends like Toni Sailer and Luis Trenker, reminiscent of the chic of
od old traditional skiing resorts, such as Sankt Anton, Sankt Moritz
d Madonna di Campiglio combined with a modern perspective on
shion and the zeitgeist of Seefeld. The identity was designed to
nvey a sense of understated luxury in a comfortable atmosphere to
sidents of the town and tourists alike.

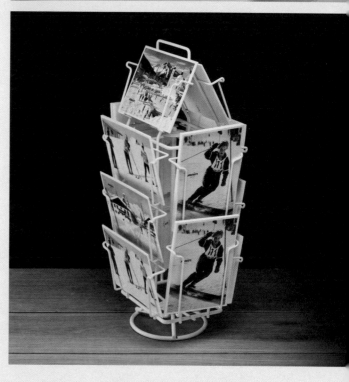

OLUTION

e developed an extensive line of stationery with Meier Seefeld's
me offset on high quality paper stock, Curious Skin (black) and Cu-
us Touch Arches (white). We furthermore created a series of ap-
cations such as wrapping paper, shopping bags, receipt folders,
e signage and bespoke accessories, such as postcards and custom
duced portable light boxes for display. For the typeface, we used
Sackers Gothic and AT Burin.

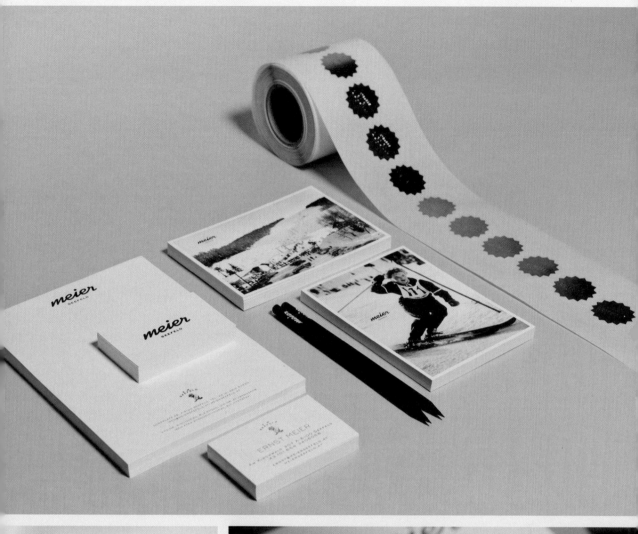

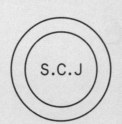

S.C.J

Gothenburg, Sweden
Design • Lundgren+Lindqvist
Photo • Cora Hillebrand
Typeface • Apercu
Paper • Rainbow grey, Greyboard

"SYMBIOSIS IS THE KEY TO GAIN TRUST OUT OF POTENTIAL CLIENTS, ESPECIALLY FOR ONE-MAN BUSINESS FOCUSED ON DESIGN."

Long-time friend and provider of Lundgren+Lindqvist's bespoke interior solution, Sebastian C. Johansson, has been designing and producing one-off interior products for some time, without a real business-oriented aim. He believed it was time to transform his rather conceptual idea of a business into something more concrete.

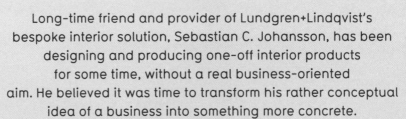

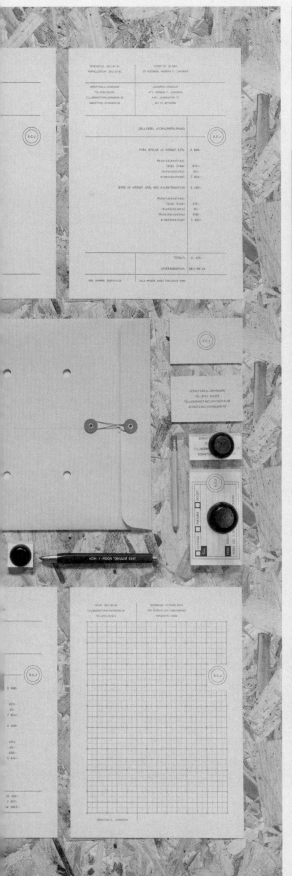

TASK

Our challenge was to define and concretise the core values of Johansson's design aesthetic in a way that would both correspond to the actual furniture and bespoke interior solutions he designs, as well as himself as a person. One important aspect was to steer him away from the often-cold façade of a bigger brand and emphasise the craftsmanship and physical nature of the products and solutions provided by Johansson.

CONCEPTION

Johansson's products are left intentionally bare, undecorated and honest with a clear focus on functionality. Often a bit 'rough around the edges', literally speaking, in materials that are usually considered inappropriate for high-end products.

The project was set to encompass strategic tasks, including the structuring of a more rigid plan for the business alongside the actual design work, and launch Johansson as both a brand and design consultant by finding a compelling way to communicate what was already there.

The notion of functionality and honesty present in Johansson's work paired with his ability to see the beauty in the simplest of all materials was something used as a starting point when designing the identity. guided the project throughout the course and informed the choices of paper stock for the stationery.

Being avid fans of mid-century modern furniture, the team was inspired by famous furniture designers' seal often applied to mark authorship. The idea, together with the expressed need for a signature that can be easily applied, led to a marque made of Johansson's initials.

SOLUTION

The fact that S.C.J is a solo practice and Johansson has no misgiving about going against convention led us to adopt a rather quirky manner, with text centred or aligned to 'flush right', for S.C.J's identity. subtle allusion to Johansson's choice of materials was also made with the use of matters like greyboard for its collateral.

The deliverables for the project include business card, letterhead invoice and quotation sheets for daily use. Other items such as blueprint template, printed tape, interdepartmental envelopes for filing and an address stamp for outgoing post were also designed for internal operations.

For Johansson's website where inspirations, making-of and finished projects are displayed, a set of avatars based on S.C.J's marque were created, allowing Johansson to publish his state of emotion as a personal and humorous touch to the brand. People of Lundgren+Lindqvist also entered Johansson's studio at Lyckholms Fabriker in Gothenburg and art-directed the photoshoot.

A company portfolio book will be due for release in 2012 spring and dispatched to the potential clients of S.C.J.

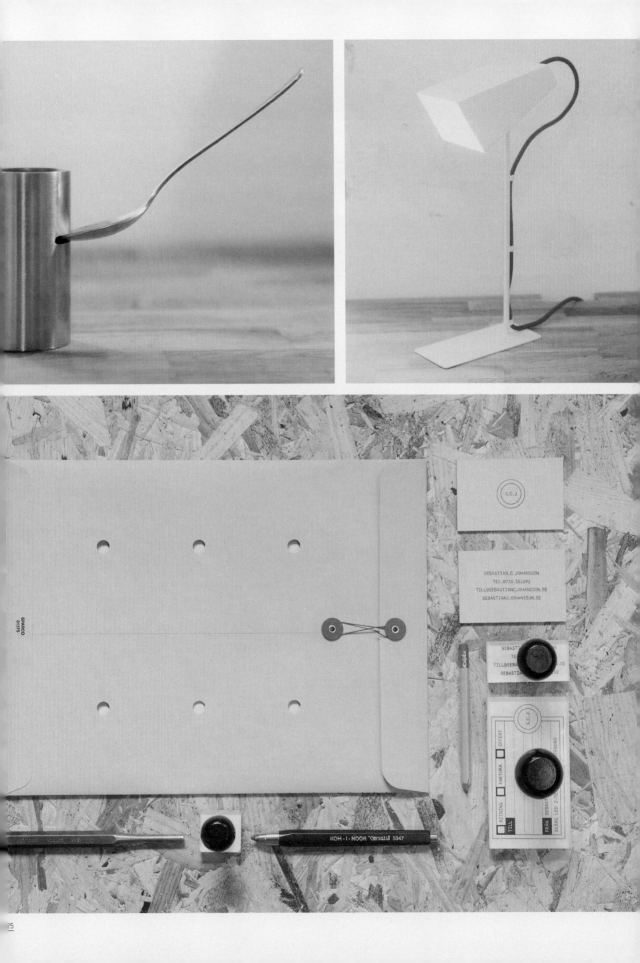

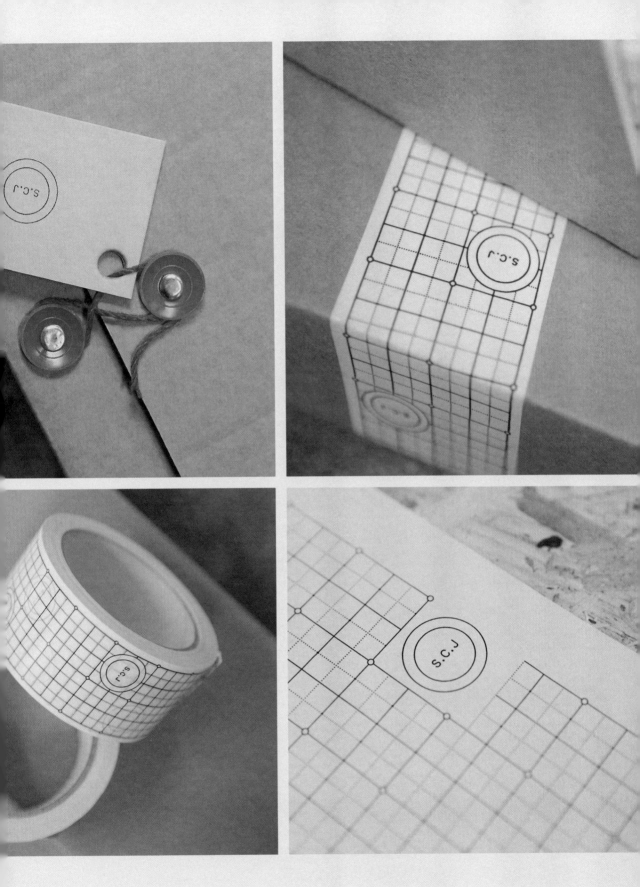

WANDERLUST

Singapore, Singapore
Design • Foreign Policy Design Group
Paper • Munken Cream, Brown Kraft, Lutece

wanderlust

"A QUIRKY
AND FUN BRAND
SYNONYMOUS WITH THE
IDEA AND EXPERIENCE
OF TRAVELS AND
JOURNEYS, THE PROCESS
OF DISCOVERY WITH
AN INNOCENT DREAM-
LIKE FEELING."

Wanderlust is a design hotel run by
Singaporean hotelier Loh Lik Peng. This hotel, located in
Singapore's Little India, targets travellers who do not
only understand and appreciate design but are curious and
interested in engaging and immersing in new experience.
Each floor of the hotel is designed by a different designer with
a free creative reign to characterise the rooms.

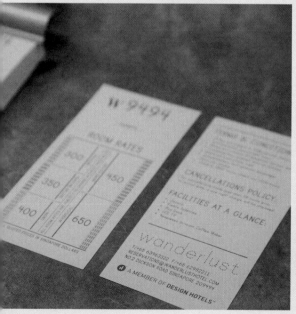

TASK

The project's goal was to create a quirky and fun brand synonymous with the idea and experience of travels and journeys, the process of discovery with an innocent dream-like feeling. The vision of the hotel owner has always been grounded by the history and surroundings of his property. Since each floor is designed by a different designer, the floors would all convey a very different look and feel. Our challenge was then to achieve a cohesive voice and unity through branding and its identity design. A voice which will also augment the ideals and creativity of the project while preserving the sense of "wanderlust".

CONCEPTION

Little India has always been an eye-opener and cultural revelation to travellers, providing that 'wanderlust' effect. We wanted to stay true to that experience by using contextual elements surrounding the area as well as from a traveller's panorama.

The building, formerly an elementary school back in the early 1900s, inspired that child-like innocence — folding a paper plane or assembling a plane kit, with the dream of possibly travelling the world one day.

Various forms of ephemera and keepsakes that could possibly be experienced during a journey were carefully studied, considered and deployed onto the collateral set to positively elevate the wanderlust experience.

SOLUTION

Foreign Policy has originated a dotted logotype for Wanderlust to express the feeling of dreaminess, fantasy and the discovery of the surreal landscape of a new world. Apart from the signage, an impulse to travel was also added to the branding, with an airmail tricolour band to enkindle the emotions and thoughts one can obtain via mails.

Standing up against the mundane, a notebook aptly identified as ITINERARY was devised as a functional and entertaining guidebook to expand and total up a traveller's voyage upon their check-in at the hotel. Besides complements, including area maps, train/bus route maps and a list of local shops and restaurants to check out in Singapore, the multi-page ITINERARY also contains blank pages for personal notes, sketches, as well as "visa stamps" to indicate arrival/departure dates, room numbers, wi-fi passwords among others that mimic immigration chops and postal stamps collectable from hotel staff.

Other items include rate cards as bus tickets, brochure as air tickets to go with an air-ticket wallet, marketing kit, signage, room service signs, room access card, room directory, tariff sheets, luggage tag, newspaper bag, hotel bag and postcards.

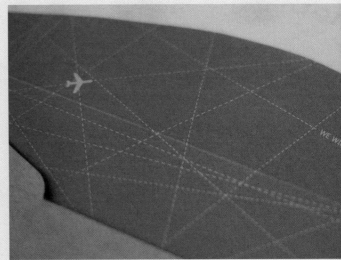

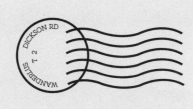

ITINERARY

CKED BAGGAGE

CHECKED BAGGAGE

3

hörst
AUTHENTISCH MANN

HÖRST

Montreal, Canada
Design • lg2boutique
Typeface • Verlag & Verlag Condensed
Paper • Mohawk Loop Antique Chalk finish, Domtar Solution

"STRATEGIC RESEARCH HELPED IDENTIFY AN OPPORTUNITY: AMONGST LARGE INTERNATIONAL PLAYERS, SEDUCTION PROVED TO BE THE MOST IGNORED PERCEPTUAL AXIS."

Formerly named 'Hörst Düsseldorf', Hörst is a designer and menswear manufacturer whose philosophy rests on the German values of impeccably-tailored cuts and quality craftsmanship which together produce a confident and inspiring style. Its high-end collection offers modern man an authentic way of being, but its poorly-defined brand positioning has led its target customers to consider it as only an overpriced mid-range line.

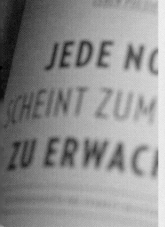

JEDE NO
SCHEINT ZUM
ZU ERWAC

STELLEN SIE ZU IHREI
PERSÖNLICHK

STETS KLASSISCH-ELEGANT
UND DOCH EXTRAVAGANT

GENIESSEN
SIE DIE FREU
DES LEBEN

OWN YOUR IDENTITY, ALWAYS CLASSY AND ELEGANT, EVEN WHEN E
ENJOY THE PLEASURES OF LIFE. NEVER SETTLE FOR EASY SEN
A STYLE THAT IS CLASSIC YET BOLD. A COMPLETELY CONFIDENT
THAT LEAVES NO ONE INDIFFERENT. NEVER ARROGANT. ALWAYS

NIEMALS
ARROGANT

hörst AUTHENTISCH

EXKLUSIVE KLEIDUNG

TASK

Hörst is a shopping devotee constantly on the lookout for that little elegant or eccentric something to reaffirm his style. He is a mature man who maintains a somewhat mysterious air. Seduction, in his view, is a game. With a slight penchant for the extravagant, he is the embodiment of the modern-day dandy.

Lg2boutique's mandate was to plan a brand strategy that would completely restyle the brand platform of Hörst. The new profile will have to produce an unmistakable image of the brand's positioning and relaunch Hörst as an upscale brand oriented to moderns.

CONCEPTION

Strategic research and the perceptual axes of the competitive field helped identify an important opportunity — amongst large international players such as Hugo Boss, Versace, Strellson, Paul Smith and Ermenegildo Zegna, seduction proved to be the most ignored perceptual axis. This insight held great potential and offered the brand a credible positioning to enter the high-end market.

SOLUTION

Directly inspired by Hörst and the brand's target wearers, the brand's emphases on authenticity are made explicit and highlighted in a "AUTHENTISCH MANN (Authentic Man)" signature recurring around the brand name on its clothing tags, prints, stationery, bags and retail fixtures that looks equally prominent as the brand itself.

Romanticism, elegance and the brand's German heritage embodied in Hörst's collection are further elaborated and envisioned in a crest and through art direction in photography on sales brochure, billboards, labels and clothing buttons in distinctive forms.

The German elements also serve as an important differentiator in a world of fashion dominated by French, Italian and British brands.

Every point of contact between Hörst and modern-day dandies has been thoroughly taken into account and manufactured to help forge a strong-yet-elegant character profile through all graphic elements for the brand.

hörst AUTHENTISCH MANN

EXKLUSIVE KLEIDUNG

hörst AUTHENTISCH MANN

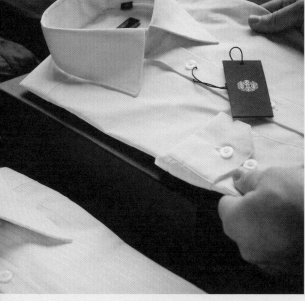

AUTHENTISCH
MANN

hörst

PERSÖN...

GENIESSEN
SIE DIE FREUDEN
DES LEBENS

NIEMALS
ARROGANT
IMMER AUTHENTISCH

09:12

Seine Gesten sind präzise
und werden mit größter Sorgfalt ausgeführt

UMFANGREICHES FACHWISSEN
DAS ULTIMATIVE KNOW-HOW

CLARIDGE'S

London, UK
Design • Construct
Typeface • SangBleu

CLARIDGE'S

"THE CHALLENGE IS ALWAYS TO KEEP THE BRAND FRESH FROM SEASON TO SEASON WITHOUT UNDERMINING THE STRENGTH OF THE OVERALL IDENTITY."

Claridge's is a five-star luxury hotel in Mayfair, owned and operated by the Maybourne Hotel Group. Its extensive and old connections with royalty have led it to being referred as an "extension to Buckingham Palace". Claridge's has been a sumptuous retreat for business travellers, stars, socialites and European royalty in a traditional London terraced house since 1812.

TASK

Construct was appointed to undertake a review of the brand positioning of Claridge's, which includes identity, communications and collateral. The initiative is part of Maybourne's long-term strategy to position the hotel for the next 100 years, ensuring the hotel remains relevant to today's travellers whilst respecting its authentic art deco heritage.

CONCEPTION

The design programme draws on Construct's experience in devising rich and diverse brand expressions as a way to involve consumers in the brand journey. The studio's reputation for this has been honed by its long-standing involvement with the luxury sector, where the challenge is always to keep the brand fresh from season to season without undermining the strength of the overall identity.

SOLUTION

Construct's extensive and ongoing design programme for this luxury Mayfair hotel expresses the hotel's main distinguishing features — an art deco heritage, timeless glamour and uniquely attentive form of traditional English service.

The hotel's crest has been redrawn and a refined version of the typeface SangBleu (Blue Blood) for the logotype has been introduced to express the hotel's heritage with elegance and restraint. It sits comfortably with the bold elements of Construct's art deco-influenced palette, with its confident colours of jade, gold, white and black, architecturally inspired chevrons, 20s-resonent typefaces and an attitude to imagery inspired by the extensive Claridge's archive.

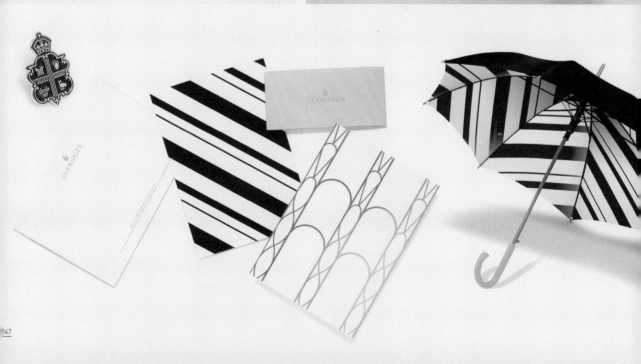

& SMITH	An independent graphic design studio based in London. Passionate about the craft and value of design, & SMITH works closely with clients to achieve a full understanding of the business, ensuring that the work they produce engages and inspires the audience. Their work encompasses corporate identity, branding, print, web solutions, book design, signage and packaging.
Anagrama	Specialising in brand development and positioning providing creative solutions for any type of project, Anagrama services reach the entire branding spectrum from strategic consulting to fine tuning brand objectives for the company to logotype, peripherals and captivating illustration design. Besides the history and experience with brand development, the agency is also an expert in the design and development of objects, spaces and multimedia projects.
Analogue	A full service graphic and digital design agency working across the arts, music, retail and leisure. Based in Leeds, UK, Analogue is proud to work with some of the most innovative and forward thinking companies from around the world.
ANTI	Short for A New Type of Interference, ANTI is a multidisciplinary design agency specialized in brand identity, art direction, packaging, print, illustration and interactive design. ANTI has a broad diversity in client experience from dairy/soft drinks, lifestyle, culture, telecom, and advertising agencies providing successful solutions on visual application and in particular online digital solutions.
ARE WE DESIGNER	With more than a decade's experience, ARE WE DESIGNER is small but efficient with more than a hundred design projects done for 56 daring and pleased clients. They always seek custom-fitted design solutions – ones that are effective and flexible, always boldly searching for what's new and budget-focused.
atipo	atipo is a small multidisciplinary studio founded in early 2010 by Raúl García del Pomar and Ismael González and based in Gijón, Spain. The background in fine arts has allowed the duo to combine different disciplines including typography, photography, painting, illustration and video, and to produce each work since experimentation.
Averill, Brogen	Averill is a graphic designer.
Barth, Greg	Currently based in Montréal, Canada, Barth is a Swiss creative and director in design, branding, typography, motion design and directing. He has worked for 7TV (Russia), Canal + (France), Ubisoft & Cirque du Soleil (Canada), ESPN, Subway, L'Oreal, Honda, Calvin Klein, etc. Barth's projects have been seen on CNN, Motionographer, Fubiz, FFFFOUND, Designsperation, and other important blogs and reference sites on the web.
BERG	An independent UK based ideas studio. Design seamlessly across a wide range of interdisciplinary media including prints, screen and the environment, BERG has an international reputation for consistently applying innovation, imagination, and sound commercial values. The team works closely with clients and industry professionals to create solutions that are considered, engaging and effective.

Bielke, Christian

Bielke is an Oslo-based graphic designer working across a broad spectrum of media ranging from concept development, visual profiling and web design, to printed media such as editorial design, books, and packaging design. Currently starting up a new firm — bielkeyang.com, with a long time business partner Martin Yang.

Bleed

Based in Oslo, Norway and Vienna, Austria, Bleed is a multidisciplinary design consultancy creating identity and experience through concept development, art direction, graphic design and service design. Representing a mix of cultures and disciplines, the team works to challenge today's conventions around art, visual language, media and identity.

Bond

A creative agency focused on branding and design for clients who value creative and practical ideas. Design means a craft for Bond, they design, visualise and define brands in a way that help companies differentiate themselves from competitions, creating brand identities, branded environments, packaging, and providing experiential web services and advertising.

Brandon, Raewyn

Brandon is a passionate web and graphic designer from New Zealand. The saying 'less is more' has highly influenced Brandon's design style as her work represents simplicity and minimalism with high attention to detail.

Bravo Company

Bravo Company is a creatively-led design studio based in Singapore. Specialising in identity, brand development, printed communications and art direction, the independent workshop works with a variety of individuals and organisations to deliver thoughtful and engaging design.

Brokstad, Daniel

Graduated in Communication Design from RMIT University, Brokstad is a freelance graphic designer, photographer and illustrator. He lived in Australia for 2 years and recently returned Stavanger, Norway.

Build

Founded in 2001, Build is a London-based graphic design consultancy. Focusing on design, art direction and identity, Build creates design solutions for a multitude of applications, media and environments with a speciality in high-end print. Build has worked on a diverse range of projects for a whole host of clients, both big and small. The studio's strength is in producing bold and memorable design and communications - Both Build, as a studio, and Michael C. Place, the husband-&-wife founder, as a solo artist, have shown works in several exhibitions in the UK and abroad, including Tokyo, Paris, New York and London.

Bureau Bruneau (Ludvig Bruneau Rossow)

The studio of Ludvig Bruneau Rossow, a graphic designer based in Oslo, Norway. Work mainly with prints, from visual identities to editorial design and packaging, Rossow believes that design should have a function and not just appears as decoration. The ideas behind his projects vary from technical to emotional concepts.

Bureau Rabensteiner

Rabensteiner is an Austrian design studio specialised in creative direction and graphic design. Since day one Rabensteiner has always been about quality and detail.

Burton, Mikey

An Ohio native, Burton proudly describes his design aesthetic as "Midwesterny" and draws much of his inspiration from artifacts found throughout the hardworking, blue collar Rust Belt: old type-specimen sheets, arcane equipment manuals and ancient textbooks. Burton has received awards from Communication Arts, Graphis, HOW, Print and, most recently, ADC Young Guns. He is now a freelancer in Philadelphia where he designs and illustrates for clients as The New York Times, The Atlantic, Newsweek, GOOD, Wired and Facebook.

clasebcn

clasebcn is a graphic design and visual communication studio in Barcelona made up of a team of young, international, multi-disciplinary professionals whose work has won a number of awards. They work on all areas of design but pay particular attention to typeface and the element of surprise.

Codefrisko

Focusing in culture and fashion, the studio is speacialised in art direction, graphic design, photography, providing online solutions, and much more. It was founded in 2006 by the founder of Frisko Design, Audrey Schayes, and the co-founder of Code Magazine Belgium, Thomas Wyngaard.

Cohen, Emanuel

Cohen is a Montreal-based multidisciplinary graphic designer graduated in 2011 from the University Quebec Montreal (UQAM), with a B.A. in graphic design and a B.F.A in design & computation arts from Concordia University in Montreal. He currently works for the Montreal-based graphic design firm Paprika.

Construct

Believing that design is intellectual, not just visual but with a sense of purpose, Construct always enjoys doing more than the brief requires. The team of no more than 10 always listens to their clients and manages projects with genuine care and obsessive attention to details.

Cornwell

Founded in 1993 by Steven Cornwell and Jane Sinclair, Cornwell is recognised by the industry as a premier Australian brand and communications agency. The award-winning studio of 30 strategy, design and account service professionals brings an insightful and strategic focus to brand-oriented business issues. In 2004, Cornwell joined the STW Group, Australia's largest communications services group to further strengthen its depth of services. 16 years since the company's inception, the brand continues to thrive and attract clients that demand a high level of strategic thinking and creative execution.

Departement

Departement is a small creative studio located in Montréal, Canada offering graphic and interactive design, web production, video directing, interactive installation and mobile production.

Deutsche & Japaner

Initiated in 2008 offering expertise in various disciplines like graphic design, product design, interior design, illustration and scenography as well as conceptual creation and strategic brand escort, the studio focuses on communication and is always in regard of sustainable experiences.

Emelyanov, Pavel

With a passion to create identity projects by using different materials, especially wood, Emelyanov now lives and works at Eskimo design studio on the far north of Russia in Murmansk.

Established	Founded in 2005 by Sam O'Donahue and Becky Jones, Established is a full-service boutique agency offering architectural, graphic and product design under one roof.
Fabio Ongarato Design	Founded in 1992 by partners Fabio Ongarato and Ronnen Goren, Fabio Ongarato Design is renowned for the diversity of its work. The studio takes an open approach to graphic design, operating across a variety of graphic disciplines, from print to exhibitions to advertising. FOD's approach to design reflects their passion for architecture, photography and contemporary art. Based in Melbourne, they work across a variety of fields such as fashion, corporate, arts and architecture deliberately crossing the boundaries between them.
Filippetti, Egidio	Born in Puglia, Filippetti studied in the European Institute of Design and is now working on graphics and visual communications for business and passion. Currently based in Spain, Filippetti has involved in individual projects and collaborations with some young Italian graphic designers such as ZagoGraphic and Viola Moroni.
filthymedia	Established in 2004, filthymedia works works across a wide range of clients and sectors, from music to fashion creating big campaigns, small projects and everything in between. Their portfolio includes graphic design, art direction, branding, typography, web & motion design, illustration, photography and copyrighting.
Finklea, Josh	Finklea is a graphic designer from Austin, Texas, who has worked and studied in Amsterdam and Los Angeles respectively, where he currently lives and received a Bachelor of Fine Arts in graphic design at Art Center College of Design.
Foreign Policy Design Group	Helmed by creative directors Yah-Leng Yu and Arthur Chin, the group works on projects ranging from creative/art direction and design, branding, brand strategy, digital strategy, strategic research and marketing campaign services for luxury fashion and lifestyle brands, fast-moving consumer goods, arts and cultural institutions as well as think tank consultancies.
Golden	A concept, branding and design agency based in Leeds, UK, Golden is headed by Creative Director, Rob Brearley, and works with clients including Nike, NBC Universal, Warner Bros., Route Publishing and somethinksounds.
Happy F&B	Established in Gothenburg in 1997 as a part of the Forsman & Bodenfors group, Happy F&B consists of people with broad expertise in branding and communication. Dedicated to all phases of the design process – from strategic analysis and forceful ideas to practical implementation, the studio creates and develops brands from entire corporate identities and packaging lines to complex single units.
Heydays	Heydays is an Oslo-based design studio that creates strong visual concepts that trigger curiosity, create excitement and show ambition. They listen, research and challenge. They remove noise to add value.

Hollands, Marcus

A graphic designer based in Brisbane, Australia, Hollands has a passion for layout and typography. He is a contributor to Californian based student design website wearefisk.com and the creator of Styles Clothing, a T-shirt company that showcases a series of six shirts each four months based on a different typeface.

Hort

Founded by Eike Koenig in 1994, Hort is a creative playground where 'work and play' can be said in the same sentence. An unconventional working environment, once a household name in the music industry, Hort is a multidisciplinary creative hub. Not just a studio space but also an institution devoted to making ideas come to life, Hort is not a client execution tool. A place to learn, to grow, and a place that is still growing, Hort has been known to draw inspiration from things other than design.

Hovard Design

The best visual communications tell stories that engage and motivate. From strategy and branding, to print design, packaging, and interactive, Hovard Design works closely with clients to craft narratives and develop the tools for their expression, from the smallest branding elements to whole communications programs. Strategic and service oriented, the team handles each project as a priority with the attention and engaged service that only a small studio can provide.

Khmelevsky, Ivan

A graphic designer from Moscow, Russia, Khmelevsky graduated from University of Hertfordshire, UK. He was an exhibition stand designer and graphic designer at Leo Burnett Moscow. He is always open for collaboration, freelance, work, parties and heavy drinking.

lg2boutique

lg2boutique, lg2 advertising's brand boutique, specialises in strategy, branding, design, packaging, printing and advertising design. In 2006, lg2 took flight, concentrating on discovering a brand's potential and telling its story. One of the most nationally and internationally recognized agencies, lg2boutique distinguishes itself by pushing every one of its clients to become leaders in their respective industries with visually compelling, strategically relevant work.

LSDK

Founded in 2009 by Christian Voegtlin and Sergej Grusdew, LSDK is a Stuttgart-domiciled design agency specialized in conceptual design, creation and communication. By intensively analyzing all relevant aspects of the existing corporate culture and especially the customer relations, LSDK develops concepts which main attribute is their individual authenticity.

Lundgren+ Lindqvist

Good design is more than ink or pixels on a surface, it is an understanding on how a message is received and experienced. By identifying the essence of that experience, Lundgren+Lindqvist creates efficient and interesting communication that is uniquely conceived for each project. The studio has a wide base of national and international clients that include a variety of corporations, media and cultural institutions. They work across many disciplines including identity design, web design and development, art direction and print design.

Manic Design

Manic Design is an award-winning creative agency with a body of work that ranges from websites and online campaigns to advertising and branding. The studio was founded in 1999 with the belief that good design always includes both creativity and communication. They for both big and small companies including international giants like BMW, Yahoo!, MINI, Starbucks, and Ford, as well as start ups and local companies.

Manifesto Futura

An independent multidisciplinary design studio based in Mexico founded in 2008, Manifesto Futura offers a variety of services and solutions for diverse customers. Specialising in art direction, brand development, and optimisation of resources, the team aims to make the best of Mexican design through clear messages and smart incentives, yet to keep the Mexican character, wit, and the charisma intact.

Manual

A design and visual communication studio based in San Francisco, California, Manual works with a broad range of clients from startups to the world's most revered brands across print, packaging, and digital media. Manual's work strives to uncover the intangible essence of a brand and express it through unique visual solutions, helping businesses and organizations articulate their unique offering, giving them more value and distinction.

Marnich Associates

Based in Barcelona, Spain, Marnich is a design and communication consultancy believing in simplicity and clarity. Their clients range from small restaurants, independent publishers and music festival to large corporations, banks and museums.

Maud

A D&AD award winning design studio based in Sydney, Australia. As passionate about the core idea as the images they create, Maud continually strives for creative excellence through consultation, collaboration and detailed execution.

moodley brand identity

moodley brand identity is an owner-led, award-winning strategic design agency with offices in Vienna, Graz and Shanghai. They believe their key contribution is to analyse complex requirements and develop simple, smart solutions with emotional appeal – whether corporate start-up, product launch or brand positioning. Established in 1999, the agency currently consists of 32 employees from 7 different countries.

Noeeko

Founded by Art and Creative Director Michal Sycz, Noeeko is a multidisciplinary design studio working across digital, print, branding and interactive media. Aim to create coherent, original and distinctive design solutions that communicate clients key messages, the team loves to experiment with new materials and techniques to keep their work fresh.

Olsen, Tom Emil

An award-winning creative director, art director and graphic designer with over 13 years of experience, Olsen has worked for both local and international clients. With various education including business marketing, advertising, graphic design, art, illustration and design, Olsen is currently located in Aalesund, Norway and works as the Executive Creative Director in Havnevik Advertising Agency.

P•A•R

A graphic design studio located in Barcelona frounded by Iris Tarraga and Lucía Castro in 2011, P·A·R offers solutions adapted to customers' needs through intense communication and strong teamwork.

Rocha, Juliano Simões da & Santos, Eduardo dos

Both graduated in Graphic Design at Universidade da Região de Joinville- UNIVILLE, Rocha has worked with many branches of graphic design while Santos is an art director in a publicity studio. They both work with a focus on visual identities.

Salikhov, Timur

An art director and graphic designer based in Saint-Petersburg, Russia, Salikhov has been involved in design, advertising and branding for 11 years and has worked with international and local clients including Unicredit, Alfa Bank, Russian Standard, Zurich Insurance, and many more. He is now working as art director for Brandson branding agency.

Studio Beige

Studio Beige is a Rotterdam-based design studio founded in 2003, specialising in concept, strategy and design with a focus on printed matter as well as web design for clients from commercial sector to non-profit organisations both large and small. The team cherishes a love for typography, which tends to show in everything they do. Unusual materials and special techniques are commonly applied to deliver striking, tactile and highly communicative designs.

Studio Lin

The NYC based graphic design practice of Alex Lin, the studio works to explore new territory through challenging collaborations with creative visionaries in the fields of architecture, industrial design, art and fashion. Their work is a highly defined rationale but not a singular style. The common denominator is a fresh, modern sensibility that eschews the overtly trendy in favor of lasting impact.

www.studiolin.org

Studio Verse

Based in Melbourne, Studio Verse specialises in print based graphic design and visual communication. With experience across a spectrum of creative and corporate fields, the team utilises a unique creative process that translates clients' messages into innovative and tailored communications, creating work that intrigues, delights and delivers, with aesthetic quality.

Studio Worldwide

Established by Dutch designer Thijs van Beijsterveldt and British designer Joe Priestland, Studio Worldwide is a multi-disciplinary design practice specialising in crafted and considered graphic design and art direction. Their clients range from arts and culture, fashion and luxury to property development and education.

Talmor, Morey

Talmor is a graphic designer from Tel Aviv, Israel, currently living and working in Brooklyn, New York. His work includes various aspects of design for printed media such as editorial design, identities, packaging design and illustration.

The Consult

A team of brand and design experts. For the past decade, The Consult has been delivering impact-making communications that strengthen brands. Understanding the market and strategic objectives is an integral part of their design process, helping to develop ideas that inspire customers and build long-lasting relationships.

Walsh, Jessica

A multidisciplinary designer living and working in NYC, Walsh has been named Computer Arts magazines "Top Rising Star in Design," an Art Directors Club "Young Gun" and Print Magazines "New Visual Artist." She has worked with studios such as Sagmeister Inc, Pentagram Design and Print magazine and freelances for a variety of clients such as The New York Times, AIGA, Computer Arts, I.D. Magazine, Technology Review, and many others.

Acknowledgements

We would like to thank all the designers and companies who have involved in the production of this book. This project would not have been accomplished without their significant contribution to the compilation of this book. We would also like to express our gratitude to all the producers for their invaluable opinions and assistance throughout this entire project. The successful completion also owes a great deal to many professionals in the creative industry who have given us precious insights and comments. And to the many others whose names are not credited but have made specific input in this book, we thank you for your continuous support the whole time.

Future Editions

If you wish to participate in viction:ary's future projects and publications, please send your website or portfolio to submit@victionary.com